D1497800

KANT

DICTIONARY

By the same author:

PLATO DICTIONARY

PLATONS WELTANSCHAUUNG

KANT-ESSAYS

KANTS ZURECHNUNGSIDEE UND
    FREIHEITSANTINOMIE

THOMAS AQUINAS DICTIONARY

DAS BUCH HIOB

MARX DICTIONARY

PHILOSOPHISCHES WOERTERBUCH

PHILOSOPHISCH-LITERARISCHE STUDIEN

KANT
DICTIONARY

MORRIS STOCKHAMMER

PHILOSOPHICAL LIBRARY
New York

"Thou, whose exterior semblance dost belie
Thy soul's immensity;
Thou best philosopher . . ."

William Wordsworth

INTRODUCTION

"God created the world for the pursuit of knowledge."

—*Kant*

Immanuel Kant (1724-1804), a philosopher's philosopher, was born in the Prussian town of Koenigsberg. As Bauer describes it, "his life was outwardly uneventful. His days proceeded with the precision of a clockwork, and he seldom left the city in which he lived, and never left his country. But from the long journeys which he undertook into the spiritual and boundless realm of human thinking, he brought back something imperishable: his philosophical works, which are among the great books of philosophy." To use Kant's standard coinage, his life was a life in or for itself: lacking an outward-empirical history, but unfolding an inner-intelligible progress. For his punctual life only mirrored the equally precise structure of his works.

The inward Kant shared the modest view of Socrates: "How many things there are which I don't need!" But he possessed that sublime humor which muses: "To be enamored of the metaphysics is my fate, although I can hardly boast of favors received from her."

According to Kant, "phenomena" are not "things-in-themselves," and vice versa. Phenomena obviously denote natural phenomena. For instance, "a house is not a thing by itself, but a phenomenon only" (CPuR). But what is a thing-in-itself? Upon the right answer to this question depends the correct interpretation of Kant's philosophical intentions.

Kant's differentiation between phenomena and things-in-themselves revolves around the dichotomy between the "is" and the

5

"ought." While phenomena or appearances signify amoral laws of nature and facts, things-in-themselves, or *noumena,* refer to spiritual laws (imperatives, commands) and to normative ideas. These moral values are "in-themselves" or original (self-determined, self-existent, unconditioned, cause-free, autonomous), i. e., inextricable from value-neuter facts.

Now, Kant's philosophic terminology can be translated into conversational parlance. Kant's fundamental thesis that noumena (things-in-themselves) are at the bottom of phenomena (appearances), means: ethical thoughts (intentions) motivate human actions. A simple truism made famous by an unusual diction. A disguising garment in which the true person can almost not be recognized.

Kant culminates a venerable philosophical tradition that was initiated by Plato and continued by Descartes, namely, the *dualism* between appearance *(res extensa)* and idea *(res cogitans).* In modern terminology we would call this the dualism between the physical or value-free event and the spiritual value. The thing-in-itself is essentially a value-idea—for instance, the command to respect one's parents, or the imperative to love one's neighbor.

Kant's assumption of spiritual or moral values, in contradistinction to the materialistic denial of them, is the *leitmotif* of his transcendental philosophy. Spiritual values *transcend* amoral natural phenomena, cannot be deduced or derived from them. "It is reprehensible to derive or limit the laws of what we ought to do according to our experience of what has been done" (CPuR). Suffice it to say that the ethical concepts of value-ideas cannot be observed, but only comprehended. This restriction is, however, no obstacle for the abstract thinker.

Kant's opinion that spiritual values are unknowable, is only a casual view; according to his final word, they can be conceived in our conceptual (inner) experience though not perceived in our sensory (outer) experience. Things-in-themselves are, therefore, not inscrutable; they can be understood. Kant's agnosticism is only transitory; he emphatically advocates an optimistic epistemology.

Now arises the question of whether those two realms of phenomena and things-in-themselves can be reconciled with one another. Kant's chief contribution to Western philosophy lies in

6

the refutation of the suspected contradiction between spiritual and natural laws: "This is the only thing which we had to do in order to remove this apparent antinomy" (CPuR). Kant's solution of his Third Antinomy proves that no logical conflict exists between moral ideas (or grounds) and amoral facts (or causes): "What is shown by this is simply this, that all things in nature and all their empirical conditions (causes) may well coexist with the presupposition of a (moral idea and of a) purely intelligible condition (moral ground), and that there is no real contradiction between these two views" (CPuR). Dualism is not inconsistent: "To conceive an intelligible (moral) ground, and to conceive it as freed from the (unfree causes), does not run counter to the unlimited empirical regressus" (CPuR). Freedom is not self-contradictory if attributed to grounds, and not to causes.

Kant's dualism, which "takes an object in two senses" (CPuR), manifests itself especially in the concept of will, that is, in the conception of two wills: the will of the law and the will of man. According to Kant's double aspect of things-in-themselves and appearances, there is also a will-in-itself (will of the law) and an appearance-will (will of man). While the latter will is causally determined, the former is causally free. Two different subjects must have different predicates. Freedom is possible if attributed to the will of the law, and not to the will of man. The novel dualism of two kinds of will is the key to freedom. (See entry on *Free Will*) "We can, without any contradiction, think the will, when phenomenal (human), as necessarily conforming to the law of nature, and so far, not free, and yet, on the other hand, when belonging to a thing by itself (to the normative law) as not subject to that law of nature, and therefore free" (CPuR). Generally speaking, matter (nature, causality) is unfree, but mind (reason, imputation) is free.

Reason and its freedom are strangers to the natural science; but they are as little abstruse to the spiritual science (ethics) as numbers to mathematics.

Successfully resolving the alleged self-contradiction of freedom, Kant did not entirely evade other inconsistencies. One would be doing Kant a disservice if one would close his eyes to some of the irreconcilable statements in his philosophical system. Kant, for instance, at the same time maintains that value-ideas exist and do not exist, that they are at once recognizable and unfathomable. One of both positions must be abandoned. Indeed, the prevalently confident Kant overcomes the occasionally skeptical double: spiritual values ultimately exist as well as physical phenomena, and can be comprehended as well as the latter. It would be unfair to consider the ephemeral as the eternal Kant. For he is an outspoken dualist (antinomist): both the moral ideas and the amoral facts are not nonexisting or nonunderstandable. Kantianism is Twoism. Vide Dualistic Philosophy.

There is still a handicap to the penetration of Kant's thoughts. For he often expresses his spiritualistic argument in a naturalistic terminology, designating the moral ground as an intelligible cause, and the imputation (moral legislation) as an intelligible causality. This misleading style, however, can be surmounted. The rediscovered Kant, then, is destined for a lasting revival.

I would like to express my thanks and appreciation to Dr. Theodore E. James of Manhattan College for his help in the arrangement of this glossary.

M. S.

ACKNOWLEDGMENTS

Grateful appreciation is extended to the publishers below for their gracious consent to the use of quotations from the following works:

Lectures on Ethics by Immanuel Kant, translated by Louis Infeld, Methuen & Co., Ltd., London, and Harper and Row, New York;

Metaphysical Principles of Virtue by Immanuel Kant, translated by James Ellington, copyright © by The Bobbs-Merrill Company, Inc., reprinted by permission of the Liberal Arts Press Division of the Bobbs-Merrill Company, Inc.;

Kant by Gabriele Rabel, by permission of Clarendon Press, Oxford;

Critique of Practical Reason by Immanuel Kant, translated by T. K. Abbott, Longmans, Green & Co., Ltd., London;

Critique of Pure Reason by Immanuel Kant, translated by F. Max Mueller, Macmillan & Co., London and New York.

Letter code following entries refers to the works below:

A   Anthropology Treated Pragmatically, Gabriele Rabel,
         translator, Clarendon Press, Oxford

BS   The Beautiful and the Sublime, Gabriele Rabel,
         translator, Clarendon Press, Oxford

CJ   Critique of Judgment
         Clarendon Press, Oxford

CPrR   Critique of Practical Reason, T. K. Abbott, translator
         Longmans Green & Co., Ltd., London

CPuR   Critique of Pure Reason, F. Max Mueller, translator
         Macmillan and Company, London and New York

DH   The Diseases of the Head, Gabriele Rabel, translator
         Clarendon Press, Oxford

DS   Dreams of a Spirit-Seer
         S. Sonnenshein & Co., London

EO   Essay on Optimism, Gabriele Rabel, translator
         Clarendon Press, Oxford

ET   The End of All Things, Gabriele Rabel, translator
         Clarendon Press, Oxford

FM   Fundamental Principles of the Metaphysics of Morals,
         T. K. Abbott, translator,
         Longmans Green & Co., Ltd., London

GTH   General Theory of the Heavens, Gabriele Rabel, translator
         Clarendon Press, Oxford

IK   Immanuel Kant, Gabriele Rabel, translator
         Clarendon Press, Oxford

KANT

DICTIONARY

A

ABSURDITY Certain absurdities find acceptance even by rational men simply because they are generally talked about.   DS.

ACCIDENTS The different determinations of a substance, which are nothing but particular modes in which it exists, are called accidents.   CPuR.

ACTION Our actions fall far short of their perfection, so that they appear blameworthy even in our own eyes—unless indeed we dull and dismiss the judge who dwells within us and who judges in accordance with it.   LE.

Action itself implies the relation of the subject of the causality to the effect.   CPuR.

Every action, so far as it produces an event, is itself an event, presupposing another state, in which its cause can be discovered.   CPuR.

The worth of actions is possible by means of the idea of spiritual value only.   CPuR.

ACTIVITY It is by his activities and not by enjoyment that man feels that he is alive. The busier we are the more we feel that we live and the more conscious we are of life.   LE.

ADMIRATION Admiration which is an affection, astonishment, can apply to things also, i.e., mountains, the magni-

13

tude, number, and distance of the heavenly bodies, the strength and swiftness of many animals, etc.   CPrR.

ADULTERY Adultery cannot take place except in marriage. For this reason adultery is cause for divorce.   LE.

ADVERSE EXPERIENCE Nothing can be more mischievous and more unworthy a philosopher than the vulgar appeal to what is called adverse experience, which possibly might never have existed, if at the proper time institutions had been framed according to those ideas, and not according to crude concepts, which, because they were derived from experience only, have marred all good intentions.   CPuR.

AESTHETICS The apparent purposefulness of a natural object that pleases us is a subjective aesthetic quality, evoked by the harmonious co-operation of imagination and intellect.   CJ.

AESTHETIC JUDGMENT Aesthetic judgments are based solely on the apparently purposeful form of the objects judged.   CJ.

AFFABILITY Affability is simply a convention of our behavior to others. It abhors anything which might give offense to them; it moderates our anger and checks any impulsive infringements of their rights; it is born of the love of mankind.   LE.

AFFECT Affects differ essentially from passions. If an affect reigns, deliberation is difficult or impossible.   MM.

AFFINITY, LAW OF The law of the affinity of all concepts requires a continual transition from every species to every other species, by a gradual increase of diversity.   CPuR.

AFFLUENCE It is not a direct duty to seek affluence for its own sake; but it may very well be an indirect duty, namely, in order to ward off poverty, which is a great temptation to vice. But then it is not my happiness, but the preservation of my moral integrity, that is my goal and at the same time my duty.   MM.

AFTERLIFE The hope of a future life rests simply on the natural disposition of every human being not to be satisfied with what is only temporal, but to feel that his true destination points higher.   CPuR. *Vide* Twofold Being.

AGE If we want to know whether a thing is very old or still young, we must not estimate it according to the number of years it has lasted, but relatively to the number of years it is expected to last. At an age at which a dog grows old, man has hardly emerged from childhood, and the oaks and cedars on Mount Lebanon have not yet reached their male prime when the lime trees or pines grow old or dry up. E.O.

AGREEABLE, THE The agreeable is based on some interest, an inclination, or a sensual desire.   CJ.

AIMS, MORAL What use can we make of our understanding, even in respect to experience, if we have not aims before us? The highest aims, however, are those of morality, and these we can only know by means of reason.   CPuR.

ALMIGHTINESS If you say, God is almighty, that is a necessary judgment, because almightiness cannot be removed, if you accept a Being, with the concept of which that other concept is identical.   CPuR.

ALMIGHTY GOD The proposition, God is almighty, contains two concepts, each having its object, namely, God and almightiness. The small word *is*, is not an additional predicate, but only serves to put the predicate in relation to the subject. CPuR.

ALTRUISM The altruistic maxim of beneficence toward those in need is a universal duty of men. MM.

AMBASSADOR Half a century ago, northern courts appointed ambassadors who, without becoming drunk themselves, could make others drunk so as to sound them out. A.

AMBITION Ambition can be characterized by vanity, or true love of honor, or both. True ambition aims at being honored for personal worth. We are all of us ambitious, but we must not push ourselves forward, because our ambitions would then miscarry. LE.

Nature demands that we should hide our ambitions, for as soon as we make a show of them we become unreasonably presumptuous. LE.

The man who saves money inordinately with a view to dissipating his hoard on show and pomp, is not miserly, but ambitious. LE.

AMENITIES The amenities do not support life, but serve to make life comfortable. LE.

AMERICA Among all people there is no nation that displays so sublime a mental character as those of North America. BS.

AMPHIBOLY, TRANSCENDENTAL Transcendental amphiboly [is] our confounding an object of the pure understanding with a natural phenomenon. CPuR.

AMUSEMENT We ought not slavishly to shun all amusement, provided we enjoy it in such a manner that we can at any time dispense with it. LE.

16

ANALOGY In philosophy, analogy does not consist in the equality of two quantitative, but of two qualitative relations, so that when two terms are given I may learn from them a priori the relation to a third only, but not that third itself. CPuR.

ANALYTICAL AND SYNTHETICAL In all theoretical judgments in which there is a relation between subject and predicate, that relation can be of two kinds. Either the predicate B belongs to the subject A as something contained in the concept A; or B lies outside the sphere of the concept A, though somehow connected with it. In the former case I call the judgment analytical, in the latter synthetical. CPuR.

ANATOMIST Although an anatomist may be convicted of error, if referring any member of an animal body to a purpose of which it can clearly be shown that it does not belong to it, it is entirely impossible in any given case to prove that an arrangement in nature, be it what it may, has no purpose at all. CPuR.

ANCIENT PHILOSOPHERS The ancient moral philosophers nearly exhausted all that can be said about virtue. RR.

ANGER Anger is a safe aid to digestion, if you can scold on lustily without fear of resistance. A.

ANIMAL Everything in an animal has its purpose. CPuR.

ANIMAL LOVE The more we come in contact with animals and observe their behavior, the more we love them, for we see how great is their care for their young. It is difficult for us to be cruel in thought even to a wolf. LE.

ANIMALS, EXISTENCE OF Animals are not self-conscious and are there merely as a means to an end. That end is man.

We can ask, 'Why do animals exist?' But to ask. 'Why does man exist?' is a meaningless question.   LE.

ANTHROPOLOGY Anthropology observes the actual behavior of human beings and formulates the practical and subjective rules which that behavior obeys.   LE.

ANTHROPOMORPHISM Anthropomorphism causes us to interpret our duties towards God by analogy with our duties towards man.   LE.

ANTICIPATION All knowledge by means of which I may know and determine a priori whatever belongs to empirical knowledge, may be called an anticipation.   CPuR.

ANTINOMY OF PURE REASON The antinomy of pure understanding exhibits the conflict between freedom and physical necessity. It was solved by showing that there is no real contradiction when the physical events are regarded [as necessitated but the intelligible noumena as free].   CPrR.

ANTITHETIC It is sad, no doubt, and discouraging, that there should be an antithetic of pure understanding, and that understanding, being the highest tribunal for all conflicts, should be in conflict with itself.   CPuR.
                        Vide Antinomy; Dialectic; Scepticism.

APOLOGY If a man shows contrition at having hurt me and is upset about it, but that does not satisfy me, it is to his honor if he apologizes. An apology is not degrading.   LE.

A POSTERIORI What is taken from experience is said to be known a posteriori or empirically only.   CPuR.
                                                Vide A priori

APPARITION However majestic and supernatural an apparition may seem to be, one must regard it as a delusion.   QuF.

APPEARANCE Appearances are called phenomena.   CPuR.
Vide Phenomenon.

APPREHENSION By the synthesis of apprehension I understand the connection of the manifold in an empirical intuition.
CPuR.

A PRIORI General truths are called knowledge a priori, while what is simply taken from experience is said to be, in ordinary parlance, known a posteriori or empirically only.
CPuR.

Logical necessity and strict universality are safe criteria of knowledge a priori, and are inseparable one from the other.   CPuR.

ARCHETYPE While the idea gives rules, the ideal serves as the archetype for the permanent determination of the copy; and we have no other rule of our actions but the conduct of that divine man within us, with which we compare ourselves, though we can never reach it.   CPuR.
Vide Wise Man

ARCHITECTONIC By architectonic I understand the art of constructing systems.   CPuR.

ARISING AND PERISHING Arising and perishing are no modifications of the substance, because the concept of modification presupposes the same subject as existing with two opposite determinations, and therefore as permanent.
CPuR.

ARMAMENT We see the various states armed to the teeth, sharpening their weapons in time of peace the one against the other. The consequences of this are such that they block our approach to the universal end of perfection.   LE.

ARMY A standing army is a cause of offensive war.   PP.

ARROGANCE Arrogance is a harmful fault. We have arrogance if we take a narrow and indulgent view of the moral law, or if the moral judge within us is not impartial. The less strict our view of the moral law and the less strictly the judge within us judges us, the more arrogant we are apt to be.   LE.

ART When we speak of a work of art, we mean a free product of human action.   CJ.

ART AND NATURE Nature is beautiful when it looks as if it might be art, and art is beautiful if, while we are conscious that it is art, it looks as free from rules as if it were nature.   CJ.

ASCETICISM The cultivation of virtue, i.e., moral asceticism, as far as the principle of the courageous, spirited, and vigorous exercise of virtue is concerned, considers the Stoic motto: Accustom yourself to bear the occasional mishaps of life and to forbear its superfluous pleasures.   MM.

ASSERTION It would really be foolish to proclaim certain bold assertions, or reckless attacks upon assertions which enjoy the approval of the largest and best portion of the commonwealth, as dangerous; for that would be to impart to them an importance which they do not possess.   CPuR.

ASSOCIATION OF THOUGHTS Explaining the association of thoughts by mechanical traces is no good, because we do not know where they meet in the brain. At times our imagination jumps so many intermediate links that we ask, 'how did I get to this?'   A.

ASSURANCE People often pronounce their views with such bold and uncompromising assurance that they seem to have abandoned all fear of error. A bet startles them. Sometimes it turns out that a man has persuasion sufficient to be valued at one ducat, but not at ten; he is ready to venture the first ducat, but with ten, he becomes aware for the first time that, after all, it might be possible that he should be mistaken. If we imagine that we have to stake the happiness of our whole life, the triumphant air of our judgment drops considerably; we become extremely shy, and suddenly discover that our belief does not reach so far.   CPuR.

ASTONISHMENT This present world presents to us so immeasurable a stage of variety, order, fitness, and beauty, whether we follow it up in the infinity of space or in its unlimited division, that even with the little knowledge which our poor understanding has been able to gather, all language, with regard to so many and inconceivable wonders, loses its vigor, all numbers their power of measuring, and all our thoughts their necessary determination; so that our judgment of the whole is lost in a speechless, but all the more eloquent, astonishment.   CPuR.

ATHEISM A man may be an atheist in theory and not in practice.
LE.

Atheism can be twofold, viz., godlessness and denial of God. Godlessness consists in not knowing God; denial of God in asserting dogmatically that there is no God.   LE.

AUTHOR It only behooves the author to propound his arguments, and not to determine beforehand the effect which they ought to produce on his judges.   CPuR.

AUTHORITY Justice and equity, the authority, not of governments, but of the conscience within us, will then rule the world.   LE.

21

AUTHOR OF THE WORLD The theist admits an author of the
world. CPuR.

People will proceed to ask, we may admit a wise and
omnipotent Author of the world? Certainly, we answer,
and not only we may, but we must. CPuR.

The belief in a great and wise Author of the world has
been supported entirely by the wonderful beauty, order,
and providence, everywhere displayed in nature. CPuR.

AUTONOMY Autonomy is the basis of the dignity of human or
rational nature. FM.

AVARICE The vice of avarice is so irrational that we would
scarcely believe it possible did we not know from experience
that it existed. Avarice swallows up all other vices: for that
very reason it is irremediable. LE.

AWE Two things fill the mind with ever new and increasing
admiration and *awe*, the oftener and the more steadily we
reflect on them: the starry heavens above and the moral
law within. CPrR. *Vide* Two Things.

AXIOM Axioms, so far as they are immediately certain, are
synthetical principles a priori. CPuR.

B

BANKNOTE Banknotes and assignats can represent money only temporarily, because it costs no labor to produce them.
MM.

BANQUET A banquet is always a temptation to immorality, namely, immoderation, to say nothing of the physical damage of overindulgence.
MM.

BEAUTY Beauty, simple and modest, is infinitely more appealing than all the arts and allurements of coquetry. It is the same with moral goodness. It is more potent and alluring in its simple purity than when it is bedecked with allurements, whether of reward or of punishment.
LE.

Why should God have made nature and its works beautiful unless it was for our contemplation?
LE.

Beauty is a symbol of morality.
CJ.

Some critics of taste mention geometrically regular figures, such as circles and cubes, as examples of beauty.
CJ.

BEAUTY OF NATURE The beauty of nature represents mere formal subjective adequacy.
CJ.

BED Bed is the nest of a host of diseases.
QuF.

23

BEGGAR The beggar at the door is often happier than the king on his throne. LE.

BEGINNING Beginning [is] happening by itself. CPuR.

BEGINNING, ABSOLUTE If you suppose that something has an absolute beginning, you must have a moment of time in which it was not. But with what can you connect that moment, if not with that which already exists? An empty antecedent time cannot be an object of perception. CPuR.

BEING Being is evidently not a real predicate, or a concept of something that can be added to the concept of a thing. It is merely the admission of a thing, and of certain determinations in it. Logically, it is merely the copula of a judgment. CPuR.

BELIEF Men like to retain the beliefs of their ancestors; for in that case their ancestors and not themselves are to be blamed for anything which may be wrong, and so long as man can transfer blame to another he is satisfied. LE.

The word *belief* refers only to the guidance which a moral idea gives me. CPuR.

I had to restrict knowledge, in order to make room for belief. CPuR.

BELIEVING If the holding true of a judgment is sufficient subjectively, but is held to be insufficient objectively, it is called believing. CPuR.

BELLIGERENCY We must put an end to that unholy belligerency on which hitherto all states have concentrated as if that were their chief end. Even if perpetual peace should remain a pious wish, we do not deceive ourselves if we try to work incessantly towards it. MM.

BELLY To keep the belly warm in cold weather is reasonable, because the bowels have to drive a nonliquid material down a long way. The body-belt worn by old people serves the same purpose. **QuF.**

BENEFICENCE Beneficence is the maxim to make the happiness of others an end for itself. **MM.** *Vide* Benevolence.

BENEVOLENCE Benevolence is the satisfaction one takes in the happiness of others. **MM.** *Vide* Beneficence.

BESTIALITY Something of the beast of prey is in all of us. **LE.**

BETTERMENT We can become better merely by altering our mode of life. **LE.**

BIBLE The practical credential of the Bible lies in the moral influence which it has always exercised on the hearts of men. The divine character of its moral content compensates for the human fallibility of the historical tale, which, like an old parchment, is illegible here and there and must be rendered intelligible by adjustments and conjectures. **QuF.**

BIGOTRY Bigotry, like sophistry, is a game, and it is far from being the same as devoutness. Bigotry is zeal in the worship of God which uses words and expressions of devotion and submission in order to win God's favor. **LE.**

BLAME If we must blame, we must temper the blame with a sweetening of love, good will, and respect. Nothing else will avail to bring about improvement. **LE.**

So long as man can transfer *blame* to another he is satisfied. **LE.**

BLAME, ACT OF LYING Although one believes that the act of lying was determined, one nevertheless blames the offender.

. . . This blame is founded on an indetermined law of reason, reason being considered as a ground which, independent of all the empirical conditions, should have determined the behavior of the man otherwise. CPuR.

BLASPHEMY If a man does not take a serious view of religion and even goes so far as to regard it as something absurd which deserves to be treated with contempt, he is a blasphemer. LE.

BODY Much depends on the body in matters of our faculty of knowledge, of our faculty of desire and aversion, and of the passions. LE.

A body in motion would, if left to itself, always follow a straight line in the same direction, which is changed however into a curvilinear motion, as soon as another force influences it at the same time in a different direction. CPuR.

BOOK A book represents a speech which someone addresses to the public by visible script. He who speaks in his own name is called the author, one who speaks in the name of the author is called a publisher. MM.

If we measured the greatness of a book, not by the number of its pages, but by the time we require for mastering it, many a book might be said to be much shorter, if it were not so short. But, on the other hand, we might be equally justified in saying that many a book would have been more intelligible, if it had not tried to be so very intelligible. CPuR.

BOOKS A student on a desert island would throw away his *books*, and search for roots instead. LE.

BOREDOM Boredom is oppressive. A.

26

BUSINESS Occupation with a purpose is business; business under difficulties is work; work is compulsory business, to which we either compel ourselves or are compelled by others.   LE.

BUSINESSMEN Businessmen tend more to greed than to miserliness.   LE.

BUSY To be constantly busy to no end is worse than not being busy at all, for it has about it an illusion of occupation.   LE. *Vide* Folly.

C

CALUMNY Calumny, by which I do not understand libel, is false defamation answerable to a court of law.   MM.

CANDID No man is in his true senses candid. Were man candid, he would have to be better constituted and to possess high principles.   LE.

A candid heart feels oppressed by having to keep its thoughts secret.   **A.**

CANNIBALISM The main difference between European and American savages lies in the fact that many members of the latter have been eaten by their foes, while the former know how to make more suitable use of their conquered enemies than to have a meal.   PP.

CARNAL Carnal purposes are those which concern the satisfaction of an inclination which is directed upon the sensible. Our trust is carnal when we ourselves determine the earthly purposes of our inclination.   LE.

CASUALTIES, MILITARY The government can call upon its subjects to fight to the death for their country, and those who fall on the field of battle are not suicides, but the victims of fate.   LE.

CATEGORICAL IMPERATIVE Act only on that maxim whereby thou canst at the same time will that it should become a universal law.

Act as if the maxim of thy action were to become by thy will a Universal Law of Nature.   FM.

Here we see philosophy in an awkward position. Its stand is meant to be firm, yet there is nothing in heaven or on earth to which it could be fixed.   FM.

CATEGORIES Categories [are] true fundamental concepts of the pure understanding.   CPuR.

Categories are concepts which a priori prescribe laws to all phenomena.   CPuR.

CAUSALITY If the empirically valid law of causality is to conduct us to the original Being, that spiritual Being must belong to the chain of objects of experience, and in that case it would, like all natural phenomena, be itself conditioned.
CPuR.

CAUSALITY, CATEGORY OF There remains the category of causality, which offers a series of causes to a given effect, enabling us to ascend from the latter, as the conditioned, to the former as the conditions.   CPuR.

CAUSALITY, PRINCIPLE OF We require the principle of the causality of the natural phenomena among themselves, in order to be able to look for and to produce natural conditions of natural events.   CPuR.

CAUSE The cause asserts, under a presupposed condition, the necessity of an effect.   CPuR.

CAUSE AND GROUND We have in us the faculty, which not only stands in connection with natural causes but is also referred to spiritual grounds.   PM. *Vide* Dualism.

CENSORSHIP This procedure of subjecting the *facts* of reason to examination, and if necessary, to blame, may be termed the censorship of reason. CPuR.

CEREMONY AND MORALITY Men think that ceremonies can take the place of morality, and they seek to win God over by nonmoral actions. If then there is absence of true religious belief, men, instead of believing that their deficiency will be made good by Heaven, have recourse to ceremonies, pilgrimages, flagellations and fastings. LE.

CERTAINTY If the faculty of imagination is not simply to indulge in dreams, but to invent and compose under the strict surveillance of reason, it is necessary that there should always be something perfectly certain, and not only invented or resting on opinion. CPuR.

Objective sufficiency is called certainty. CPuR.

CHANGE Change is a mode of existence, which follows another mode of existence of the same object. Hence whatever changes is permanent, and its condition only changes. CPuR.

CHARACTER However capable and talented a man may be, we still ask about his character. However great his qualities, we still ask about his moral quality. LE.

Since character works by principle, the evils in character can be gradually eradicated by good principles, until no natural disposition to wickedness has control over it. LE.

Persons who are passing judgment on others often reveal their own character. CPrR.

CHARITY Charity is a duty which we owe to mankind and in the last analysis it is a question of right. LE.

Charity is a thing apart where right and justice are concerned. LE.

CHASTITY A virtue with regard to its sensuous impulse is called chastity. MM.

CHEATED Nature wisely implanted in human beings a propensity for being cheated. A.

CHEATING To cheat is to make a lying promise, while a breach of faith is a true promise which is not kept. A lying promise is an insult to the person to whom it is made, and even if this is not always so, yet there is always something mean about it. LE.

CHEERFULNESS One should do everything cheerfully, even dying; for everything loses its value, if done in a grumbling or sulking mood. A.

CHERISHING If he can cherish a passion for my sweetheart, he can equally cherish a passion for my purse. LE.

CHILDREN A child accustomed to command in the home grows up dictatorial, meets in life with all kinds of resistance to which it is unaccustomed, and find itself unfitted for society. LE.

Children share their sweets only so long as they have enough and to spare. LE.

A child must play, must have his hours of recreation; but he must also learn to work. OE.

CHOICE That choice which is determined by pure reason is called free choice. MM.

CHURCH We do not enter a church to serve God there: we do so in order to prepare ourselves to serve Him in our lives. We must carry out in practice outside the church the preparations we have made within it, and so devote our lives to God's service.   LE.

CIRCLE The common definition of a circle, that it is a curved line every point of which is equally distant from one and the same point, is faulty, because the determination of *curved* is introduced unnecessarily.   CPuR.

CIVILIZATION The more civilized man becomes, the broader his outlook and the less room there is for special friendships; civilized man seeks universal pleasures and a universal friendship, unrestricted by special ties; the savage picks and chooses according to his taste and disposition, for the more primitive the social culture the more necessary such associations are.   LE.

How is civilized man to be trained both for nature and for civil society? For the education of man in respect to his natural and civil conditions are the two ends of nature.
                                                    LE.

As men become more civilized, they become also better actors. They pretend to feel affection, respect, modesty, unselfishness, but deceive no one.   A.

CIVILIZED MAN The savage reaches *manhood* as soon as he is capable of propagating his species, but not the civilized man; civilized man must not only be able to propagate his species, but to maintain himself and his children.   LE.

CLEARNESS Clearness is not, as the Logicians maintain, the consciousness of a representation; for a certain degree of consciousness, though insufficient for recollection, must exist, even in many dark representations. A representation is clear in which the consciousness is sufficient for a consciousness of its difference from others.

CPuR. Vide Darkness.

CLERGYMAN Clergymen occasionally prophesy the total decay of religion, and they do just what is required to this end by teaching observances instead of moral principles.　　QuF.

COEXISTENCE, CAUSE AND EFFECT In coexistence, cause and effect exist at the same time. There may be, for instance, inside a room heat which is not found in the open air. If I look for its cause, I find a heated stove. But that stove, as cause, exists at the same time with its effect, the heat of the room, and there is therefore no succession in time between cause and effect, but they are coexistent.　CPuR.

COGNITION An objective sensation is called cognition. Cognition is either intuition or concept.　　　　　　　　CPuR.

COHABITATION The goal of nature in the cohabitation of the sexes is procreation, i.e., preservation of the race.　　MM.

COLOR Colors are not qualities of a body, though inherent in its intuition, but they are modifications only of the sense of sight, as it is affected in different ways by light.　　CPuR.

COMFORT To live in too great comfort and pamper oneself results in weakness and languor.　　　　　　　QuF.

We may enjoy in stormy weather, when comfortably seated in our warm, cosy parlor, speaking of those at sea, for it heightens our own feeling of *comfort*.　　　LE.

It is true that it is a hardship to live in want after one has tasted the joys of comfort.　　　　　　　　　　　LE.

Contentment is negative; comfort is positive. All comforts

and pleasures should be enjoyed in such a way that we can dispense with them; we ought never to make necessities of them. LE.

COMMANDS Everybody looks upon moral laws as commands. CPuR.

Commands are laws which must be obeyed, that is, must be followed even in opposition to inclination. FM.

COMMON MAN Common men are those whose worth is of that degree which can be expected from every one; they have no merit and are not worthy of honor; they deserve respect and esteem, but not honor and deference. Integrity, honesty, and punctilious discharge of our obligations may be expected from all of us; these qualities entitle us to respect, but not to honor and homage. LE.

COMMON SENSE A man of common sense is a metaphysician without knowing it. MM.

What is sound sense? It is the common sense, so far as it judges rightly. But what is common sense? It is the faculty of the knowledge and use of rules in concreto, as distinguished from the speculative understanding, which is a faculty of knowing rules in abstracto. PM.

It is indeed a great gift of God, to possess plain common sense. But to appeal to common sense, when insight and science fail, and no sooner—this is one of the subtle discoveries of modern times, by means of which the most vapid babbler can safely enter the lists with the most thoroughgoing thinker, and hold his own. PM.

COMMUNION If we can unburden our heart to another, we achieve complete communion. That this release may be achieved, each of us needs a friend, one in whom we can confide unreservedly, to whom we can disclose completely all our dispositions and judgments, from whom we can and need hide nothing, to whom we can communicate our whole self. LE.

COMMUNITY The schema of community or of the reciprocal causality of substances is the coexistence of the determination of the one with those of the other. CPuR.

COMPLAINING Complaining and whimpering, even merely crying out in bodily pain, are unworthy of you, especially when you are aware that you deserve pain. MM.

COMPLIMENT Compliments and every courtesy, gallantry, even with the most fervent declarations of friendship, deceive nobody. A.

COMPREHENSION In comprehending any object under a concept, the representation of the former must be homogeneous with the latter, that is, the concept must contain that which is represented in the object to be comprehended under it, for this is the only meaning of the expression that an object is comprehended under a concept. CPuR.

COMPROMISE In our syncretistic age a certain shallow and dishonest system of compromise of contradictory principles is devised, because it commands itself better to a public which is content to know something of everything and nothing thoroughly, so as to please every party. CPrR.

COMPULSION Compulsion there must be, but not slavish compulsion. LE.

Subjective compulsion is the determination of a person by that in himself as Subject which has the greatest determining and moving force. LE.

CONCEPT No knowledge is possible without a concept, and a concept is always, with regard to its form, something general, something that can serve as a rule.   CPuR.

If there were no lower concepts, there could not be higher concepts.   CPuR.

CONCEPT AND EXISTENCE Whatever our concept of an object may contain, we must always step outside it, in order to attribute to it existence.   CPuR.

CONCEPT OF REASON Concepts of reason are not derived from nature.   CPuR.

CONCILIATION Once planted, the seed would grow; once propagated, conciliation would maintain itself by public opinion.   LE.

CONCILIATORY The man who abhors dissension and discord and is ready to accommodate himself to the sentiments of others, so long as no moral issue is involved, is conciliatory and one need not fear a quarrel with him.   LE.

CONCUPISCENCE Concupiscence is to be distinguished from appetite itself as being the stimulus for the determination of appetite. Concupiscence is a sensuous mental state that has not yet turned into an act of the faculty of appetite.
          MM.

CONDITION It follows from the very concept of the conditioned that through it something is referred to a condition, and, if that condition is again conditioned, to a more distant condition.   CPuR.

CONDUCT [We are] demanding from reason nothing but the rule of our *conduct*.   CPuR.

CONFESSION If force is used to extort a confession from me, if my confession is improperly used against me, and if I cannot save myself by maintaining silence, then my lie is a weapon of defense. LE.

CONFLICT OF DUTIES A conflict of duties is that relationship between them in which one would annul the other. MM.

CONJUNCTION All conjunction is either composition or connection. CPuR.

CONNECTION Connection is representation of the synthetical unity of the manifold. CPuR.

I soon found that the concept of the connection of cause and effect was by no means the only one, by which the understanding thinks the connection of things. PM.

CONSCIENCE Conscience is an instinct to pass judgment upon ourselves in accordance with moral laws. It is not a mere faculty, but an instinct; and its judgment is not logical, but judicial. LE.

Conscience is the representative of the forum divinum. LE.

Two things fill the mind with ever new and increasing admiration and awe, the oftener and the more steadily we reflect on them: the starry heavens above and the moral law within. I have not to search for them and conjecture them as though they were veiled in darkness or were in the transcendent region beyond my horizon; I see them before me and connect them directly with the consciousness of my existence. The former begins from the place I occupy in the external world of sense, and enlarges my connection therein to an unbounded extent with worlds and systems of systems, and moreover into limitless times of their periodic motion, its beginning and continuance. The second begins from my invisible self, my personality, and exhibits me in a world which has true infinity, but which is traceable only by the understanding, and with which I discern that I am not in a merely contingent but in a universal and necessary connection, as I am also thereby with all those visible worlds. The former view of a countless multitude of worlds annihilates as it were my importance as an *animal* creature, which after it has been for a short time provided with vital power, one knows not how, must again give back the matter of which it was formed to the planet it inhabits. The second on the contrary infinitely elevates my worth as an *intelligence* by my personality, in which the moral law reveals to me a life independent of animality and even of the whole sensible world, at least so far as may be inferred from the destination assigned to my existence by this law, a destination not restricted to conditions and limits of this life, but reaching into the infinite. CPrR.

CONSCIOUSNESS The consciousness of my own existence is, at the same time, an immediate consciousness of the existence of other things. CPuR.

The consciousness of oneself is, with all our internal perceptions, empirical only, and always transient. CPuR.

CONSEQUENCE The consequences must flow right from the assumed ground. Logic.

CONSEQUENCE AND EFFECT *Vide* Dualistic Philosophy.

CONSISTENCY Consistency is the highest obligation of a philosopher, and yet the most rarely found. CPrR.

CONSPIRACY If there were not wretched traitors in every conspiracy, entire states would soon be overthrown. A.

CONSTITUTION They admit that 'the best constitution is that in which not man but laws are in power.' MM.

The true character of a constitution is often concealed. QuF.

A constitution founded on the greatest possible human freedom of each individual to exist by the side of the freedom of others, is a necessary idea, on which not only the first plan of a constitution or a state, but all laws must be based. CPuR.

A good constitution is not to be expected from morality, but, conversely, a good state of a people is to be expected only under a good constitution. PP.

CONSTRUCTION By constructing a concept I mean representing a priori the intuition corresponding to it. CPuR.

CONTEMPT It hurts one more to be treated with contempt than to be hated. A contemptible man is a universal object of disdain; no one holds him in regard, and he loses all sense of his own value. LE.

CONTENTMENT Is it not possible to have peace and content- ment, great though our wretchedness and trouble may be? We might be sad and yet content without feeling that we ought to thank God for our lot. Not our senses but our reason might recognize that the ruler of the world does nothing without purpose. Thereby we find consolation in, though not for, the evils of life, a solid contentment with the course of life as a whole. LE.

If we are content with little it is no hardship to do without things, and we can live happily. LE.

CONTEST Both parties beat the air and fight with their own shadows, because they go beyond the limits of nature,

where there is nothing that they could lay hold of with their dogmatical grasp. They may fight to their hearts' content, the shadows which they are cleaving grow together again in one moment, like the heroes in Valhalla, in order to disport themselves once more in these bloodless contests.
CPuR.

CONTINGENT The contingent exists only under the condition of something else as its cause. CPuR.

CONTINUUM As every number must be founded on some unity, every phenomenon, as a unity, is a quantum, and, as such, a continuum. CPuR.

CONTRADICTION If we take single passages out of their connection, and contrast them with each other, it is easy to pick out apparent contradictions, particularly in a work written with all the freedom of a running speech. CPuR.

CONTRADICTION, PRINCIPLE OF The proposition that no subject can have a predicate which contradicts it, is called the principle of contradiction. It is a general though only negative criterion of all truth, and belongs to logic only, because it applies to knowledge as knowledge only, without reference to its object, and simply declares that such contradiction would entirely destroy and annihilate it.
CPuR.

It is impossible that anything should be and at the same time not be. For instance, a man who is young cannot be at the same time old, but the same man may very well be young at one time and not young, that is, old, at another.
CPuR.

CONVERSATION Man has a great liking for conversation. LE.

When we attend to the course of conversation in

41

mixed companies, consisting not merely of learned persons and subtle reasoners, but also of men of business or of women, we observe that, besides story telling and jesting, another kind of entertainment finds a place in them, namely argument, for stories if they are to have novelty and interest are soon exhausted, and jesting is likely to become insipid.

CPrR.

CONVERSION A man who changes his religion and goes over from the religion of his parents and ancestors to another is counted foolhardy. He is thought to be committing a very dangerous act since thereby he takes all blame upon himself.

LE.

Some old people conceive the notion of becoming converted towards the end of their lives and think they can thereby make amends for all past misdeeds and place themselves in the same position as if they had lived morally all their lives. Such people consider sudden death as the greatest misfortune.

LE.

CONVICTION If the judgment is valid for everybody, if only the person is possessed of reason, then the ground of it is objectively sufficient, and the holding it to be true is called conviction.

CPuR.

COPERNICUS Copernicus, not being able to get on in the explanation of the movements of the heavenly bodies, as long as he assumed that all the stars turned round the spectator, tried, whether he could succeed better, by assuming the spectator to be turning round, and the stars to be at rest.

CPuR.

COQUETRY Coquetry debauches instead of commending itself, and when ethics plays the flirt she courts the same fate.

LE. *Vide* Beauty.

CORRELATIVE The present state, points to an antecedent state. as a correlative of the event that is given.   CPuR.

CORRUPTION The more corrupt the moral concepts, the more corrupt are the theological concepts.   LE.

COSMOLOGY The system of all phenomena is the object-matter of cosmology.   CPuR.

COUNSELS Counsels depend on whether this or that man reckons this or that as part of his happiness.   FM.

COUNTRY In a small country the boundaries are nearer and there seem to be more of them. For a small country it is more important to defend its own possessions than to set out blindly upon new conquests.   DS.

COURAGE The faint-hearted who complain about their luck and sigh and weep about their misfortunes are despicable in our eyes; instead of sympathizing with them we do our best to keep away from them. But if a man shows a steadfast courage in his misfortune, and though greatly suffering, does not cringe and complain but puts a bold face upon things, to such a one our sympathy goes out.   LE.

Where there is courage, there is reverence for the humanity in one's own person.   MM.

COURTESY Of my friends I require, not advantage, but the joy of their company and the opportunity to open my heart to them; but courtesy I require from everyone. Courtesy signifies a pleasantness sufficiently fine to enable us to please others in the smallest trifles.   LE.

COWARDICE Man's cowardice dishonors humanity. It is cowardly to place a high value upon physical life. The man who on every trifling occasion fears for his life makes a

laughingstock of himself. We must await death with
resolution. LE.

CREATION Only the noumena can be said to have been created
by God: God is not a creator of appearances. CPrR.

CREATURE Nothing in a creature is futile or purposeless. CJ.

CRITIC Instead of rushing in, sword in hand, it is far wiser to
watch the struggle from the safe seat of the critic. That
struggle is very hard for the combatants themselves, while
to you it need not be anything but entertaining, and, as the
issue is sure to be without bloodshed, it may become highly
improving to your own intellect. In this dialectical war no
victory is gained that need disturb your peace of mind.
CPuR.

CRITICISM Understanding in all its undertakings must submit
to criticism, and cannot attempt to limit the free exercise
of such criticism without injury to itself, and without ex-
posing itself to dangerous suspicion. There is nothing so
important with reference to its usefulness, nothing so sacred,
that it could withdraw itself from that searching examination
which has no respect of persons. The very existence of
understanding depends on that freedom; for understanding
can claim no dictatorial authority, but its decrees are rather
like the votes of free citizens, every one of whom may
freely express, not only his doubts, but even his veto.
CPuR.

To deny that this service, which is rendered by
criticism, is a *positive* advantage, would be the same, as to
deny that the police confers upon us any positive advantage,
its principal occupation being to prevent violence, which
citizens have to apprehend from citizens, so that each may
pursue his vocation in peace and security. CPuR.

44

If we consider the invincible obstinacy of the dogmatical sophists, who are deaf to all the warnings of criticism, there really seems nothing left but to meet the boasting on one side by an equally justified boasting on the other, in order at least to startle reason by a display of opposition, and thus to shake her confidence and make her willing to listen to the voice of criticism. CPuR.

CRITIQUE Our critique is meant to form a necessary preparation in support of a thoroughly scientific system of metaphysics. CPuR.

Whenever I hear that some uncommon genius has demonstrated away the freedom of the human will, the hope of a future life, or the existence of God, I am always desirous to read his book, for I expect that his talent will help me to improve my own insight into these problems. The opponent of religion would give me a valuable opportunity for amending here and there the principles of my own *critique of pure reason*, while I should not be at all afraid of any danger arising from his theories. CPuR.

CRYING Crying is feminine, in a man effeminate. A man who has a tear shining in his eye can be forgiven. But he must not let it drop and it is unforgivable if he accompanies it with the odious music of sobbing. A.

CULTURE Culture is intended to form a certain kind of skill, without destroying another kind which is already present. CPuR.

CURIOSITY Nothing would be more prejudicial to the enlargement of our knowledge than that curiosity which, before entering upon any researches, wishes to know beforehand the advantages likely to accrue from them, though quite unable as yet to form the least conception of such advantages, even though they were placed before our eyes. CPuR.

45

CUSTOM In matters of custom I must follow others.   LE.

CYNIC The Cynic is the ideal of innocence, or rather of simplicity. Diogenes taught that the highest good is to be found in simplicity, in the sober enjoyment of happiness.   LE.

D

DEATH All men, even the unhappiest and the wisest, have a natural fear of death. **A.**

We must await death with resolution. **LE.**

Would not an uninterrupted increase of vital force beyond a certain degree lead to death from joy? **A.**

DEATH, DESIRE OF If you hear a long-suffering hospital patient assert how he longs for death to relieve him from his ordeal, don't believe him; he is not serious. **QuF.**

DEATH, FEAR OF Fear of death frequently works an improvement in us, but we are at a loss to say whether we are improved or converted. Would the improvement have taken place if death were not in sight and we had hopes of longer life? **LE.**

DEBTOR To be indebted is to be subject to an unending constraint. I must for ever be courteous and flattering towards my benefactor, and if I fail to be so he will very soon make me conscious of my failure; I may even be forced to using subterfuge so as to avoid meeting him. But he who pays promptly for everything is under no constraint. **LE.**

DECEIT Deceit destroys all confidence. **LE.**

DECORUM Decorum is a graceful illusion. **A.**

DEED A deed is a free action which falls under the law.   LE.
Vide Imputation.

DEFINITION To define means only to represent the complete concept of a thing within its limits and in its primary character.   CPuR.

A very important prudential rule, viz., not to rush into definitions, and to attempt or pretend completeness or precision in the definition of a concept, when one or other of its characteristic marks is sufficient without a complete enumeration of all that constitute the whole concept. CPuR.

DEFOLIATION Repeated defoliation kills the tree.   CJ.

DEIST AND THEIST Those who admit a transcendental theology only are called Deists, those who admit also a natural theology Theists. The former admit that we may know the existence of an original Being by mere reason. The latter maintain that reason is capable of determining that object more accurately in analogy with nature.   CPuR.

DEMOCRACY Democracy is necessarily despotic, because it establishes an executive power in which all decide over one.   RR.

DEMONSTRATION An apodictic proof only, so far as it is intuitive, can be called demonstration.   CPuR.

DEPRECIATION It is easier to depreciate another than to emulate him, and men prefer the easier course.   LE.

DESIGN As much of design as you discover in the world, so much of confirmation has the legitimacy of your idea received.   CPuR.

DESIRE The more artless and simple our desires the less likely are we to go astray in satisfying them.   LE.

I cannot know, except by experience, what desires there are which are to be satisfied, nor what are the natural means of satisfying them. CPuR.

DESIRE, DETERMINING PRINCIPLE OF The determining principle of the desire is based on the feeling of pleasure and pain. CPrR.

DESTRUCTION OF NATURE A propensity to the wanton destruction of beautiful though lifeless things in nature is contrary to man's duty to himself. MM.

DESTRUCTIVENESS Destructiveness is immoral; we ought not to destroy things which can still be put to some use. No man ought to mar the beauty of nature; for what he has no use for may still be of use to some one else. LE.

DETERMINATION As soon as man is impelled to act, all this play of the speculative theory vanishes like the phantoms of a dream. CPuR.

DETERMINATION IN NATURE No power of nature can, of its own accord, deviate from its own laws. CPuR.

DETERMINATION, PRINCIPLE OF Every concept is, with regard to that which is not contained in it, undetermined and subject to the principle of determination, according to which of every two contradictory opposite predicates, one only can belong to it. This rests on the principle of contradiction. CPuR.

DEVOUTNESS Devoutness is an indirect relation of the heart to God, which seeks to express itself in action. LE.

DIALECTIC There exists a natural and inevitable Dialectic of pure understanding, not one in which a mere bungler might get entangled from want of knowledge, or which a sophist might artificially devise to confuse rational people, but one that is inherent in, and inseparable from, human understanding, and which, even after its illusion has been exposed, will never cease to fascinate our understanding, and to precipitate it into momentary errors, such as require to be removed again and again. CPuR.

DIETETICS Dietetics is the art of preventing diseases, in contrast to therapeutics which is the art of curing them. QuF.

DING AN SICH (THING IN ITSELF) We must admit and assume behind the appearance something else that is not an appearance, namely, the thing in itself. FM.

DISCIPLINE Discipline implies compulsion; but as compulsion is opposed to freedom and freedom constitutes man's worth, the compulsion of discipline must be so applied to the young that their freedom is maintained. LE.

That our temperament and various talents which like to indulge in free and unchecked exercise require some kind of *discipline*, will easily be allowed by everybody. CPuR.

The trees in the forest *discipline* each other; they cannot obtain air for growth in the space between them, but only up above, and so they grow tall and straight; but a tree in the open is not restricted and so grows crooked, and it is then too late to train it. So it is with man. Trained early, he grows up straight along with his fellows; but if he is never pruned, he becomes a crooked tree. LE.

Discipline must precede doctrine. Discipline cultivates heart and temperament, while character is rather cultivated by doctrine. Discipline is correction. Man must be disciplined, because he is by nature raw and wild. LE.

The restraint which checks our constant inclination

to deviate from certain rules, and at last destroys it, is called discipline. CPuR.

DISCONTENT Discontent with one's condition under a pressure of many anxieties and amidst unsatisfied wants might easily become a great temptation to transgression of duty. FM.

DISCURSIVE The knowledge of every understanding must be by means of concepts, not intuitive, but discursive. CPuR.

DISCUSSION What people may differ about it is not the matter so much as the tone and manner of these discussions. CPuR.

DISGUST Anyone can see that an action is disgusting, but only the man who feels disgust at it has moral feeling. The understanding sees that a thing is disgusting and is hostile to it, but it cannot be disgusted: it is only the sensibility which is disgusted. LE.

DISINGENUOUSNESS There is in human nature a certain disingenuousness. There is no doubt that this tendency to conceal oneself and to assume a favorable appearance has helped towards the progress of civilization, nay, to a certain extent, of morality, because others, who could not see through the varnish of respectability, honesty, and correctness, were led to improve themselves by seeing everywhere these examples of goodness which they believed to be genuine. CPuR.

DISPOSITION, GOOD To perform an action without a good disposition is to comply with the letter of the law but not with its spirit. LE.

DISPOSITION If we do a thing with a liking, we do it from a good disposition. LE.

51

DISPUTE How can two persons dispute on a subject the reality of which neither of them can present either in real, or even in possible experience, while they brood on the mere idea of it with the sole intention of eliciting something more than the idea, namely, the reality of the object itself? How can they ever arrive at the end of their dispute, as neither of them can make his view comprehensible and certain, or do more than attack and refute the view of his opponent? CPuR.

DISSENTER We call a man a dissenter if, while not differing from us in matters of practical importance, he takes a different view on some speculative points of religion. We may consider that he is wrong, but that is no reason why we should hate him, and we are lovers of peace only if we avoid hostility towards dissenters. LE.

DIVERSITY It is only under a presupposition of a diversity in nature, and under the condition that its objects should be homogeneous, that we have understanding, because it is this very diversity of all that can be comprehended under a concept which constitutes the use of that concept. CPuR.

DIVINE BEING A concept of the Divine Being was elaborated which we now hold to be correct, not because natural science has convinced us of its correctness, but because it fully agrees with moral principles of reason. CPuR.

DIVINE JUSTICE Divine justice must reward good conduct and punish bad with unerring precision. LE.

DIVISION OF LABOR All trades, arts, and handiworks have gained by division of labor, namely, when, instead of one man doing everything, each confines himself to a certain kind of work distinct from others in the treatment it requires, so as to be able to perform it with greater facility and in the greatest perfection. FM.

DOGMATISM Dogmatism is the dogmatical procedure of pure understanding, without a previous criticism of its own power. CPuR.

Accustomed as he is to dogmatism, he swallows the poison which destroys his principles by a new dogmatism. CPuR.

Popular interest is entirely on the side of dogmatism. CPuR.

Dogmatism gives to every question an answer with a full stop. CPuR.

DOING Man's worth must be measured by what he does. LE.

What a man does not do willingly, he does poorly. ET.

Man judges that he can do a certain thing because he is conscious that he ought to do it. CPrR.

DOLE If man earns his bread, he eats it with greater pleasure than when it is doled out to him. LE.

DOUBT Who raises the doubt, must expect opposition from all sides. PM.

Man is more inclined to doubt and to investigate than to approve and acknowledge; he finds it safer to postpone judgment. This tendency has its roots in the understanding, and also in the fact that we wish to guard against error. Yet to close all the approaches to knowledge is the way to ignorance. LE.

DREAM If each man has his own world, we can surmise that he dreams. DS.

If the antecedent phenomenon were there, and the event did not follow on it necessarily, it would become to me a mere play of my subjective imagination, or if I thought it to be objective, I should call it a dream. CPuR.

DRESS Provided that a brave and industrious man dresses passably well, provided that he does not show himself quite indifferent to and ignorant of how to dress, but dresses as befits his station in life and in the fashions of his time, he is more respected than is the man who is effeminate in his ways and foppish in dress. LE.

DRINKER Jolly drinkers dislike it if one person remains sober at a carousal, watching their foibles while restraining his own. A.

DROP OUT Everybody knows with what zeal and alacrity volatile youth frequents the courses in the beginning, and how later the lecture rooms become more commodious. IK.

DRUGS Opium and other vegetable products cause for a while a dreamy euphoria and freedom from care, and even an illusory strength. But they are harmful in that afterwards depression and weakness follow; worst of all, there results a need to take these stupefying agents in ever increasing amounts. MM.

DRUNKARD A drunkard who gives up drink because of the harm it does to him will ultimately acquire the habit of sobriety and will come to see that it is better to be temperate than to be a drunkard. LE.

DUALISM In respect to mere perception and receptivity of sensation man must reckon himself as belonging to the world of sense, but in respect to pure activity in him he must reckon himself as belonging to the intellectual world. FM.

Our criticism was true, in teaching us to take an object

in two senses, namely, either as natural phenomenon, or as thing by itself. CPuR.

All phenomena in space are represented as totally different from the acts of thought. CPuR.

DUALISTIC CONSISTENCY There is not the smallest contradiction in saying that a natural phenomenon or a thing in appearance is subject to certain laws, from which a moral idea or a thing in itself is independent. FM.

DUALISTIC PHILOSOPHY (Twoism) There are two roots of human knowledge, viz. sensibility and understanding. CPuR.

Even thinkers by profession did not clearly distinguish between the two elements of our knowledge, the one being in our possession completely a priori, the other deducible a posteriori. CPuR.

To know a thing as an object is possible under two conditions. First, there must be intuition by which the object is given us, secondly, there must be a concept by which an object is thought as corresponding to that intuition. CPuR.

Our criticism was true, in teaching us to take an object in two senses, namely, either as a natural phenomenon, or as a moral thing in itself (noumenon). CPuR.

The legislation of human understanding (philosophy) has two objects, nature and freedom (free morals), and contains therefore both the law of nature and the law of morals. CPuR.

We can conceive two kinds of causality, causality either of nature or of freedom (free morals). CPuR.

The causality may be considered from two sides, as intelligible, and as sensible. CPuR.

This twofold way of conceiving the faculty of an object does not contradict any of the concepts which we have to form.
CPuR.

According to this we should have in every subject of the world of (human) sense, first, an empirical character. Secondly, we should have to allow to it an intelligible character also.
CPuR.

With reason we find a rule and order, totally different from the order of nature.
CPuR.

Reason does not follow the order of things, as they present themselves as natural phenomena, but frames for itself a new order according to moral ideas.
CPuR.

These actions have taken place, not because they were determined by empirical causes, but by the unempirical causes of reason.
CPuR.

Hence a rational being has two points of view from which he can regard himself: first, so far as he belongs to the physical world of sense; secondly, as belonging to the intelligible (supersensuous or moral) world.
FM.

Man is destined for two entirely different worlds.
QuF.

It is not to be wondered at that man, as belonging to both worlds, must regard . . .
CPrR.

Two things fill the mind with ever new and increasing admiration . . . The first (thing) begins . . . The second begins . . . The first view . . . The second view . . .
CPrR. Vide: Necessity, philosophy, world.

DUTIES Purposes which are duties are: one's own perfection and other people's happiness, not one's own happiness and other people's perfection. MM.

DUTY Duty is that action to which a person is obligated. MM.

The majesty of *duty* has nothing to do with enjoyment of life; it has its special law and its special tribunal, and although one would like to shake them well together, in order to give them, mixed, like medicine, to the sick soul, they will soon separate of themselves, and if they do not the former will not act; and although physical life might gain somewhat in force, the moral life would fade away irrevocably. CPrR.

Duty is the necessity of acting from respect for the law. FM.

A ruler does not care whether his subjects' obligations towards him are discharged from duty or compulsion: it is all the same to him; but parents demand that children should fulfil their obligations towards them from duty. LE.

DUTY AND RIGHT To every duty there corresponds a right. MM.

DUTY TO ONESELF My duty towards myself cannot be treated juridically; the law touches only our relations with other men; I have no legal obligations towards myself; and whatever I do to myself I do to a consenting party; I cannot commit an act of injustice against myself. LE.

DYNAMICAL RELATIONS The three dynamical relations from which all others are derived, are inherence, consequence, and composition. CPuR.

57

E

EARTH The advantage which arises from the circular shape of the earth is well known; but few only know that its flattening, which gives it the form of a spheroid, alone prevents the elevations of continents, or even of smaller volcanically raised mountains, from continuously and, within no very great space of time, considerably altering the axis of the earth. The protuberance of the earth at the equator forms however so considerable a mountain, that the impetus of every other mountain can never drive it perceptibly out of its position with reference to the axis of the earth. And yet people do not hesitate to explain this wise arrangement simply from the equilibrium of the once fluid mass.
CPuR.

If I have got so far as to know that the earth is a sphere and that its surface is spherical, I am able from any small portion of it, for instance, from a degree, to know definitely and according to principles, the diameter, and through it, the complete periphery of the earth; and, though I am ignorant with regard to the objects which are contained in that surface, I am not so with regard to its extent, its magnitude, and its limits.   CPuR.

ECONOMY It is a bad economy to spend blindly whatever comes in and not to be able to determine, when there is a stoppage, which part of the income can bear the expenditure, and where reductions must be made.   CPuR.

It is merely a subjective law of economy, applied to the stores of our understanding; having for its purpose, by means of a comparison of concepts, to reduce the general use of them to the smallest possible number.   CPuR.

EDIFICATION Edification is the effectual working of devoutness, the perfecting of an effective, practical disposition of the heart to act in accordance with the will of God.   LE.

EDIFICE We found that although we had thought of a tower that would reach to the sky, the supply of materials would suffice for a dwelling house only, sufficiently roomy for all our business on the level plain of experience, and high enough to enable us to survey it; and that the original bold undertaking could not but fail for want of materials, not to mention the confusion of tongues which inevitably divided the laborers in their views of the building, and scattered them over all the world, where each tried to erect his own building according to his own plan.   CPuR.

EDUCATION Man can only become man by education.   OE.

Man is the only being who needs education.   OE.

The state has no money left to pay efficient teachers who perform their job with gusto, because the state needs everything for its wars.   QuF.

Wherein lies our hope? In education, and in nothing else. Education must be adapted to all the ends of nature.   LE.

All education must be free, so far as the pupil does not interfere with the freedom of others.   LE.

From its earliest infancy we ought to instil in the child an immediate hate and disgust of hateful and disgusting actions.   LE.

60

Since in early youth it cannot be known what ends are likely to occur to us in the course of life, parents seek to have their children taught a great many things, and provide for their skill in the use of means for all sorts of arbitrary ends.   FM.

EFFECT At the moment in which an effect first arises it is always coexistent with the causality of its cause, because if that had ceased one moment before, the effect would never have happened.   CPuR.

EFFEMINACY Excessive self-indulgence in comfort is effeminacy. The prevalence of effeminacy completely saps our human strength.   LE.

EGO It is the permanent and unchanging Ego which forms the correlative of all our representations, if we are to become conscious of them.   CPuR.

EGOISM Egoism can be logical, aesthetical, or practical.   A.

EGOIST, LOGICAL The logical egoist likes 'to be different' and enjoys paradoxes.   A.

ELDERLY The old are fond of saying that things don't happen as they ought to.   LE.

Elderly people who are miserly live longer than if they were not miserly; to save money they live temperately, they would not be so temperate if it cost money; they show how good their digestion is by the way they eat and drink when some one else pays the bill.   LE.

ELEGANCE We show elegance when our coarsenesses have been rubbed away. We scrape and polish one another until we fit together satisfactorily. Thus arises tact, which manifests

61

a refinement in our power of judging what is pleasing and displeasing to others. LE.

EMBELLISHMENT All embellishments of the mind are its luxuries; they appertain to the melius esse, but not to the esse of it. LE.

EMOTION Some strong emotions prompt health mechanically. This is chiefly true of laughing and crying. A.

Emotion belongs to feeling, which makes reflection more difficult or even impossible. MM.

EMPIRICAL EXPERIENCE It is quite possible that even our empirical experience is a compound of that which we receive through impressions, and of that which our own faculty of knowledge supplies from itself. CPuR.

EMPIRICAL JUDGMENTS The relation of cause and effect forms the condition of the objective validity of our *empirical judgments*. CPuR.

EMPIRICAL LAW Empirical laws exist and are discovered through experience. CPuR.

EMULATION Emulation, not imitation, is what an exemplary author should provoke in others. CJ.

END The 'final end' is not of such a kind that amoral nature by itself can achieve it. Only in man as a subject of morality do we find the final end. CJ.

Essential ends are not as yet the highest ends; in fact, there can be but one highest end. We must distinguish, therefore, between the ultimate end and subordinate ends, which necessarily belong, as means, to the former. CPuR.

The means derive all their value from the *end*.   CPrR.

END IN ITSELF Rational nature exists as an end in itself. So act as to treat humanity, whether in thine own person or in that of any other, in every case as an end withal, never as a means only.   FM.

ENEMY Some confidence in the character of the enemy must be retained even in the midst of war.   PP.

We can have either an honest or treacherous enemy. The fawning, clandestine, deceitful enemy is far baser than the open one, even though the latter be violent and wicked. We can defend ourselves against the latter, but not against the former.   LE.

ENEMY, UNJUST What is an unjust enemy, when every state is judge in its own cause? An enemy whose maxim, if it were taken as universal law, would render all peace among nations impossible.   MM.

ENJOYMENT Mere enjoyment leads to weariness of life; but to die having had fullness of life is possible only after a life of action, and after we have made such full and busy use of our life that at its end we are not sorry that we have lived.   LE.

ENMITY To bear a man ill will is definitely to wish him harm, and as enmity postulates both dislike and ill will, a disposition to be pleased when ill befalls others, we ought to cherish enmity against none.   LE.

ENTHUSIASM Nothing great can be achieved without enthusiasm.   CJ.

ENVY To grudge a man his share of happiness is envy. To be envious is to desire the failure and unhappiness of another not for the purpose of advancing our own success and happiness but because we might then ourselves be perfect and happy as we are. LE.

EPICUREANS The Epicureans set up the ideal of prudence. LE.

EQUALITY All men are equal, and only he who has superior morality has superior intrinsic worth. LE.

EQUAL RIGHT The world is an arena on which nature has provided everything necessary for our temporal welfare, and we are nature's guests. We all have an *equal right* to the good things which nature has provided. Every one of us, therefore, in enjoying the good things of life must have regard to the happiness of others. LE.

EQUALS The propositions that if equals be added to equals the wholes are equal, and if equals be taken from equals the remainders are equal, are really analytical, because I am conscious immediately of the identity of my producing the one quantity with my producing the other. CPuR.

ERROR No error exists in our knowledge, if it completely agrees with the laws of our understanding. CPuR.

Single errors may be corrected by censure, and their causes removed by criticism. CPuR.

ESTEEM Esteem regards the inner worth, love only the relative worth of our fellows. We are esteemed for our intrinsic worth. LE.

The less inner worth a man has, the less *esteem* does he deserve. LE.

ETHICS Ethics is sometimes described as the theory of virtue. LE.

EUTHANASIA, MORAL If eudamonism is taken as the principle instead of eleutheronomy, the consequence is the euthanasia of all morality. MM.

EVENT The event, as being conditional, affords a safe indication of some kind of condition, while that condition itself determines the event. CPuR.

EVIL Moral badness is always accompanied by physical. RR.
Vide Punishment; Moral and Physical.

EVIL SPIRIT If we believe that evil spirits can have an influence upon us, can appear and haunt us at night, we become a prey to phantoms and incapable of using our powers in a reasonable way. LE.

EXAMPLE On the whole examples are desirable. Their absence gives us an excuse. LE.

An example is not for copying, but for emulation.
LE. *Vide* Mathematics.

It is the one great advantage of examples that they sharpen the faculty of judgment, but they are apt to impair the accuracy and precision of the understanding, because they fulfil but rarely the conditions of the rule quite adequately. Nay, they often weaken the effort of the understanding in comprehending rules according to their general adequacy, and independent of the special circumstances of experience, and accustom us to use those rules in the end as formulas rather than as principles. Examples may thus be called the gocart of the judgment, which those who are deficient in that natural talent can never do without. CPuR. *Vide* Illustration.

EXERCISE Lack of exercise extinguishes vitality, while too vigorous exercise can exhaust. QuF.

EXISTENCE We may analyze as much as we like, we shall never arrive from one object and its existence at the existence of another, or at its mode of existence by means of the concepts of these things only. CPuR.

Vide Dualistic Philosophy.

EXPECTATION If the imagination is aroused, the expectation will mostly be disappointed. A.

EXPEDIENTS All expedients which take us off our guard are thoroughly mean. Such are lying, assassination, and poisoning. LE.

EXPERIENCE I am conscious by means of external experience of the reality of bodies, as external phenomena in space, in the same manner as I am, by means of my internal experience, of the existence of my soul. PM.

What *experience* teaches me under certain conditions, it must always teach me and everybody, and its validity I do not limit to the subject. PM.

Experience is no doubt the first product of our understanding, while employed in fashioning the raw material of our sensations. Nevertheless, experience is by no means the only field to which our understanding can be confined. Experience tells us what is, but not that it must be necessarily as it is and not otherwise. It therefore never gives us any really general truths. CPuR. *Vide* Dualism.

Experience, though it teaches us that after one phenomenon something else follows habitually, can never teach us that it follows necessarily. CPuR.

Experience, as a kind of knowledge, requires understanding. CPuR.

With regard to nature, it is experience no doubt which supplies us with rules, and is the foundation of all empirical truth: with regard to moral laws, on the contrary, experience is, alas! but the source of illusion; and it is altogether reprehensible to derive or limit the laws of what we ought to do according to our experience of what has been done. CPuR.

How can we make out by experience, whether the world is from eternity or had a beginning? PM.

EXPERIMENT We experiment with human beings also, as when, for instance, we test a servant to see if he is honest. LE.

Of what use would it be to define an empirical concept, as for instance that of water, because, when we speak of water and its qualities, we do not care much what is thought by the word, but proceed at once to experiments? CPuR.

EXPLANATION 'To explain' something means to derive it from clearly understood premises. CJ.

EXTERMINATION A war of extermination, in which the destruction of both parties and of all justice can come about, would occasion perpetual peace only in the vast burial grounds of the human race. PP.

EXTERNAL SENSE By means of our external sense, we represent to ourselves objects as external or outside ourselves, and all of these in space. CPuR.

EXTRAVAGANCE The imagination may perhaps be forgiven for occasional extravagance. But the understanding which ought to think can never be forgiven for substituting extravagance. PM.

F

FACULTY Everything that is founded in the nature of our faculties must have some purpose, and be in harmony with the right use of them, if only we can guard against a certain misunderstanding and discover their proper direction.
CPuR.

FAITH The firmest faith needs not to fear the severest test of reason.
CPuR.

Faith stands in no need of logical demonstrations, but is itself justified in postulating its content as a necessary hypothesis.
LE.

There is only one religion, but there can be faiths of several kinds.
RR.

FANATICISM Fanaticism exceeds all limits of the maxims of reason.
LE.

FAULT They recognize their faults, and think that all men have such faults that none is able to do anything good.
LE.

FAULTFINDING Once faultfinding begins between friends their friendship will not last long. We must turn a blind eye to the faults of others, lest they conclude that they have lost our respect and we lose theirs. Only if placed in positions of authority over others should we point out to them their defects.
LE.

FAVOR Men are ashamed by favors. If I receive a favor, I am placed under an obligation of the giver. We all blush to be obliged. Noble-minded men accordingly refuse to accept favors.   LE.

FEAR Fear of God is not rooted in his goodness, but in His unerring justice. God must be feared as a just judge. To fear God is not the same as to be afraid of Him. We are afraid of God when we have transgressed and feel guilty, but we fear Him when we are so disposed to conduct ourselves that we can stand before Him.   LE.

Fear of God can be filial or slavish.   LE.

FEAST A feast has beyond the mere physical well-being also a moral purpose in view, namely, to bring many people together for a long time in mutual communication.   MM.

FEDERATION The feasibility of the idea of federation, which should gradually spread to all states and thus result in perpetual peace, can be proved.   PP.

FEELING Feeling is not a faculty of representing things, but lies outside the whole field of our powers of cognition. CPuR.

A man can have feeling and inclination for something without having emotion and passion.   LE.

Tender feelings towards dumb animals develop humane feelings towards mankind.   LE.

FEMALE SEX When nature entrusted her most precious pledge to the female lap, by which the species was to be perpetuated, she was anxious to protect it and implanted that anxious timidity and fear of bodily injury into female nature, which rightly expects to be protected by masculine strength.   A.

FERVOR, RELIGIOUS The most ungodly of all passions is that of religious fervor, because it makes man think that under the cloak of piety he can do all manner of things.   LE.

FICTION Fictions [are] quite indemonstrable.   CPuR.

FIRST MOVER   *Vide* God.

FLATTERER A flatterer is not always a liar; he is merely lacking in self-esteem, he has no scruple in reducing his own worth and raising that of another in order to gain something by it.   LE.

FLATTERY There exists a form of flattery which springs from kindness of heart. Some kind souls flatter people whom they hold in high esteem. There are thus two kinds of flattery, kindly and treacherous. People who are not given to flattery are apt to be faultfinders.   LE.

FOLLY Busy folly is the characteristic of our species. We see people hastily starting good schemes but not sticking to them; we see them building only to demolish. Good and evil seem to neutralize each other, resulting in empty fussing about, so that all the doings on our globe appear as a mere farce.   QuF.

FORM That which causes the manifold matter of the natural phenomenon to be perceived as arranged in a certain order, I call its form.   CPuR.

The philosophers of antiquity considered all form in nature as contingent, but matter, according to the judgment of common understanding, as primitive and necessary. CPuR.

FORTITUDE Fortitude is the capacity and resolved purpose to withstand a strong but unjust opponent.   MM.

FORTUNE Wealth in excess is a fortune; to have a fortune is more than to have means. A man who has a fortune does not need others and does not require their help. In the second place, fortune is power; it has purchasing power; it enables us to procure all that can be produced by human powers.   LE.

FRAILTY, HUMAN Man's frailty causes him to transgress the law, and his weakness makes his actions fall short of its purity.   LE.

FRANKNESS Frankness, by which we mean the combination of candor and affability, is very popular.   LE.

FREEDOM Beings, who have received the gift of *freedom*, are not content with the enjoyment of comfort granted by others.   QuF.

That this [third] antinomy rests on a mere illusion, and that nature does not contradict the freedom of *moral* grounds, that was the only thing which we could prove, and cared to prove.   CPuR.

Vide Freedom and Necessity; Ground, intelligible.

FREEDOM, POLITICAL Freedom is the inner value of the world, but on the other hand, freedom unrestrained by rules of its conditional employment is the most terrible of all things. I can conceive freedom as the complete absence of orderliness, if it is not subject to an objective determination. Therefore the proper use of freedom is the supreme rule.   LE.

That freedom, the principle of the highest order of life, should annul itself and abrogate the use of itself conflicts with the fullest use of freedom. But freedom can only be in harmony with itself under certain conditions; otherwise it comes into collision with itself. If there were no estab-

lished order in nature, everything would come to an end, and so is it with unbridled freedom, private or political.
LE.

In the unregulated pursuit of an inclination, man becomes an object of utter contempt, because his freedom makes it possible for him to turn nature inside out in order to satisfy himself. Let him devise what he pleases for satisfying his desires, so long as he regulates the use of his devices; if he does not, his freedom is his greatest misfortune. Freedom must therefore be restricted, though not by other properties or faculties, but by itself.
LE.

Just as freedom is the source of virtue which ennobles mankind, so is it also the root of the most dreadful vices. . . . The use of freedom must be in keeping with the essential ends of humanity.
LE.

One thing is quite certain, namely, that it is useful to grant to reason the fullest freedom, both of enquiry and of criticism, so that she may consult her own interest without let or hindrance. And this is done quite as much by limiting her insight as by enlarging it.
CPuR.

It is part of that freedom that we should be allowed openly to state our thoughts and our doubts which we cannot solve ourselves, without running the risk of being decried on that account as turbulent and dangerous citizens.
CPuR.

FREEDOM AND CAUSALITY In this way freedom and nature exist together and without any conflict, according as we refer it to the intelligible ground or to the sensible cause.
CPuR. *Vide* Ought.

If we want to save freedom, no other way remains but to attribute causality to the appearance and freedom to the thing in itself. This is certainly inevitable, if we like to

retain both these contradictory concepts as compatible with
one another. CPrR.

FREEDOM AND LAW OF NATURE Freedom of reason is no
hindrance to the natural law of physical phenomena, neither
does this law interfere with the freedom of reason, which
is connected with things in themselves, as moral grounds.
We thus rescue freedom, and do not curtail natural necessity. PM.

FREEDOM AND NECESSITY Our problem was, whether freedom is contradictory to natural necessity: and this we have
sufficiently answered by showing that freedom has relation
to a very different kind of conditions from those of nature,
so that the law of the latter does not affect the former,
and both exist independent of, and undisturbed by, each
other. CPuR. *Vide* Coexistence; Dualism.

How can a man be called quite free at the same moment,
and with respect to the same action in which he is subject to an inevitable physical necessity? CPrR.

FREEDOM FROM CAUSES It is possible to affirm freedom in
spite of the natural mechanism of actions as natural phenomena. CPrR. *Vide*

Pure or timeless reason, as a simple intelligible faculty, is
not subject to the form of time, or to the unintelligible
conditions of the successions of time. CPuR.
Vide Reason; Imputation.

The spiritual condition that lies in reason is not sensuous,
and therefore does itself not begin. Thus we get what we
missed in all empirical series of conditions, namely, that
the condition is itself empirically unconditioned. For here
the condition is really outside the series of natural phe-

nomena, and therefore not subject to any sensuous cause.

CPuR. *Vide* Pure Reason.

Could the action of reason be called free in that case, as it is accurately determined by the empirical character and rendered necessary by it? CPuR. *Vide* Ought; Blame.

Freedom must be the foundation of all moral laws and the consequent responsibility. CPrR.

If things in themselves were nothing else but natural phenomena, freedom could not be saved. CPuR.

The clear consciousness of freedom was produced by the clear exhibition of free duties in opposition to all the claims of unfree sensuous desires. CPuR.

FREEDOM OF WILL All men attribute to themselves freedom of will. Hence come all judgments upon actions as being such as ought to have been done although they have not been done. FM.

The proof for freedom of the will from mechanism is based on the subtle difference between the normative will of the law (free) and the psychological will of man (unfree).

CPuR.

If we could investigate all the manifestations of the human will to the very bottom, there would be not a single action which we could not predict with certainty and recognize from its preceding causes as necessary. There is no freedom therefore with reference to this empirical or amoral character. . . . If, however, we compare caused actions with free reasons, with reference to moral purposes, we find a physically unnecessary rule and intelligible order, totally different from the order of nature. For, from this point of view, everything, it may be, ought not to have happened according to spiritual grounds, which according to the course of nature has happened, and according to its empirical causes, was inevitable.   CPuR.

Vide Freedom and Causality.

If we want to save freedom, there is no other way than to realize that it has its seat in the nonsensuous moral subject.
CPrR.

FREE LAW Freedom and an unconditional practical law reciprocally imply each other.   CPrR.

FREETHINKER Where is this so-called freethinker to take the knowledge that there exists no Supreme Being? This proposition lies outside the field of possible experience and, therefore, outside the limits of all human cognition. CPuR.

FREE WILL The human will is an *arbitrium liberum* [free will]. However much, for instance, we may try by torture to force a man to action we cannot compel him to do it if he does not will it; if he so will he can withstand every torment and not yield.   LE.

Vide Self-compulsion; Freedom of Will.

The will is an *arbitrium liberum* [free will], because sensuous impulses do not necessitate its actions, but there is in it a faculty of determination, independent of the necessitation through sensuous impulses.   CPuR.

A will which is independent of sensuous impulses, and can be determined by motives presented reason alone, is called Free will.   CPuR.

A will which can have its law in nothing but the mere legislative form of the maxim is a free will.   CPrR.

Since the principle of causality applies to things only, if

taken in the first sense, namely, so far as they are objects of experience, but not to things, if taken in their second sense, we can, without any contradiction, think the will when phenomenal as necessarily conforming to the causal law of nature, and so far, not free, and yet, on the other hand when belonging to a thing by itself, as not subject to that will of nature, and therefore free.   CPuR.

Vide the Introduction; Dualism.

FRIENDSHIP If I know and can assume with confidence that my friend will really help me in need, I have a true friend. LE.

The maximum reciprocity of love is friendship, and friendship is an idea because it is the measure by which we can determine reciprocal love.   LE.

If men complain of the lack of friendship, it is because they themselves have no friendly disposition and no friendly heart. They accuse others of being unfriendly, but it is they themselves who, by demands and importunities, turn their friends from them.   LE.

Because of the rarity of true friendship we must guard against repeatedly calling upon a friend to help us out of our difficulties lest we become a burden to him and give him the impression that our calls upon him may be never-ending.   LE. *Vide* Selfishness.

A man without a friend is isolated. Friendship develops the minor virtues of life.   LE.

FRUGALITY We must be frugal in eating and in drinking. The vices of overeating and overdrinking are bestial and degrade man.   LE.

FUN For a joke, a boy will stick a pin in an unsuspecting playmate, but it is only for fun. He has no thought of the pain

77

the other must feel on all such occasions. In the same spirit he will torture animals; twisting the cat's tail or the dog's. LE.

FUTURE LIFE The hope of a future life has chiefly rested on that peculiar character of human nature, never to be satisfied by what is merely temporal. CPuR.

FUTURE WORLD We cannot penetrate the secrets of the other world. If you are avid for more information, have patience until you get there. DS.

G

GAMBLING Why is gambling so entertaining? Because it is a continual alternation between fear and hope. Afterwards supper tastes better and is more invigorating.   **A.**

GAMES All our evening parties demonstrate how enjoyable playing can be, for almost none of them can entertain without games.   **CJ.**

GENERAL TRUTH General truths, which at the same time bear the character of an inward or logical necessity, must be independent of experience,—clear and certain by themselves.   **CPuR.**

GENERATIO HOMONYMA What experience shows is always generatio homonyma, which means that the offspring is of the same kind as the parent.   **CJ.**

GENEROSITY Generosity is a superfluity. A man who is never generous but never trespasses on the rights of his fellows is still an honest man, and if everyone were like him there would be no poor in the world.   **LE.**

GENIALITY Geniality, courtesy, politeness and civility are simply virtue manifesting itself in small things.   **LE.**

GENIUS Genius is the natural gift which sets the rules of art.   **CJ.**

GENUS Every genus requires species, and these again sub-species.
CPuR.

GEOGRAPHY I present a physical and a *moral geography*. It describes the interconnection between lands and sea and those things which influence trade and commerce. Without this foundation history differs little from fairy-tales. The second part considers man throughout the earth and distinguishes what is moral in him. When we compare different sorts of men and consider the moral conditions of earlier times, a great map of the human race unfolds itself before our eyes. IK.

GEOMETRY Geometry is a science which determines the properties of space. CPuR.

GLUTTONY Gluttony is lower than drunkenness in that it is occupied with sense as a passive condition, and not with active imagination. MM.

In so far as it serves sociability, immoderate drinking, although a bestial vice, is not as contemptible as gluttony; the latter is far baser, because it neither promotes sociability, nor does it enliven the body, but is purely bestial. LE.

Immoderation in the consumption of food and drink is misuse of the means of nourishment. MM.

GOAL I can indeed be forced by another person to actions which are conceived as means to a goal, but I can never be forced by him to have a goal; I alone can make something a goal for myself. MM.

GOD Every one imagines God in terms of that concept which is most familiar to himself. We may, for instance, imagine Him as a great and mighty lord, something beyond the mightiest of the lords of this earth. LE.

Any false idea about God makes morality immoral.   CJ.

It is now easy to find the answer to the weighty question, whether the notion of God is one belonging to physics or to morals.   CPrR.

No one will be able to boast that he knows by sensuous experience that there is a God. For a man who knows that, is the very man whom I have been so long in search of. . . . No, that conviction is not a logical, but a moral certainty.
                                                                              CPuR.

If I call God the first mover that does not help me in the least to recognize what God is.   CJ. *Vide* Predicates.

GODLESSNESS Of a practical atheist one must be able to say that he is godless, for godlessness is a kind of shameless wickedness which defies the fear of punishment which the representation of God inspires in us.   LE.

GOLDEN AGE All make the world begin from good; with the golden age, with life in paradise.   RR.

GOLDEN RULE We must do to others as we require that they should do to us.   LE.

GOOD AND EVIL The German language has the good fortune to possess expressions which do not allow this difference to be overlooked. It possesses two very distinct concepts and especially distinct expressions, which the Latins express by a single word, *bonum*. For *bonum* it has "das Gute" [moral good], and "das Wohl" [amoral well, psychological weal], for *malum* "das Boese" [moral evil], and "das Uebel" [amoral ill, physical evil], or "das Weh" [physical woe]. So that we express two quite distinct judgments when we consider in an action the *good* and *evil* of it, or our *weal* and *woe*.   CPrR. *Vide* Meaning.

GOOD CAUSE Where the public has once persuaded itself that certain subtle speculators aim at nothing less than to shake the very foundations of the common welfare of the people, it is supposed to be not only prudent, but even advisable and honorable, to come to the succor of what is called the good cause, by sophistries, rather than to allow to our supposed antagonists the satisfaction of having lowered our tone to that of purely practical conviction, and having forced us to confess the absence of all speculative and apodictic certainty. I cannot believe this, nor can I admit that the intention of serving a good cause can ever be combined with trickery, misrepresentation, and fraud.   CPuR.

GOOD MAN Nowadays naming someone a good man is the same as calling him stupid.   DH.

GOODNESS Moral goodness endues man with an immediate, inner, absolute moral worth.   LE.

GOOD WILL Nothing can possibly be conceived in the world which can be called good without qualification, except a Good Will.   FM.

GOVERNMENT So far no government has contributed one iota to the perfection of mankind, to inner happiness, to the worth of humanity; all of them look ever and only to the prosperity of their own countries, making that their chief concern.   LE. *Vide* Ruler.

When the government slackens its reins a little, sad consequences happen.   QuF.

Governments ordain not dispositions, but only actions. LE.

GRACES Social graces are only externals, giving a fair virtuous appearance which, however, deceives nobody. They are small change indeed.   MM.

GRACIOUSNESS Graciousness is the beauty of virtue.   BS.

GRAMMAR He who speaks without knowing grammar, speaks according to rules although he is unaware of it.   Logic.

GRASS The inner structure of a mere blade of grass is only conceivable as ruled by a purpose.   CJ. *Vide* Intention.

GRATIFICATION Young man! Refrain from the gratification of saturating yourself with entertainment, orgies, love, etc. —not with the Stoical intent of renouncing them altogether but in the finer Epicurean desire to have in prospect a constantly increasing delight.   A.

It is more painful to have to forego gratifying a desire because it is not in our power to gratify it, than to forego gratification when we could gratify it if we wished. The mere possession of the power of gratification is pleasant.
     LE.

GRATITUDE We are grateful not only for what we have received but also for the good intention which prompted it, and the greater the effort it has cost our benefactor, the greater our gratitude.   LE.

Gratitude is merely an ethical, and not a legal, obligation.
     MM.

GRAVITY The laws of gravity, determining the movement of the heavenly bodies, imparted the character of established certainty to what Copernicus had assumed at first as an hypothesis only.   CPuR.

GREAT INTELLIGENCE If we have once postulated a Great Intelligence, why should we not also provide it with all imaginable perfections? In this manner the moral mainsprings of the mind are stirred up, a lively interest is strengthened by rhetorical power, and a strong and to a large extent even wholesome illusion arises.   CJ.

GREEK PHILOSOPHY Ancient Greek philosophy was divided into three sciences: Physics, Ethics, and Logic. This division is perfectly suitable to the nature of the thing.   FM.

GROUND Empirical grounds are divided from the senses, in so far as the senses find satisfaction in them. Intellectual grounds are those in which all morality is derived from the conformity of our actions to the laws of reason.   LE.

The consciousness of purposiveness is a consciousness of a ground.   CJ.

GROUND, INTELLIGIBLE To conceive an intelligible ground of moral phenomena, and to conceive it as freed from the causality of causes, does not run counter to the unlimited empirical regressus in the series of natural phenomena. And this is really the only thing which we had to do in order to remove this apparent antinomy.   CPuR.
Vide Third Antinomy; Intelligible Ground.

GROUND AND CAUSE Moral grounds represent not a reference to amoral causes in the natural phenomenon. . . . We may consider the former as free, but the latter as subject to natural necessity.   PM. *Vide* Dualistic Philosophy.

GRUDGE Grudge is the displeasure we feel when another has an advantage; his advantage makes us feel unduly small and we grudge it him.   LE.

GUARDIAN A cold-blooded but well-disposed guardian, advocate, or patriot, is a man of cool deliberation who will resolutely do his utmost for our good.   LE.

GUILT A criminal lying under sentence of death frets and worries and reproaches himself severely, but mainly for the imprudence which led to the detection. He imagines that it is his conscience which reproaches him for his immorality; but it is not the pangs of conscience that he feels; for, had he got off scot-free, he would have felt no qualms, and if he had a conscience he would feel its reproach in any event.   LE.

Men have yet invariably felt themselves more guilty in their own eyes than in the eyes of God.   LE.

GULLIBLE No reproach is more bitter to the philosopher than that of being *gullible* and a victim of common illusion. It is cheap to sneer at the sage when things are equally incomprehensible to him as to the ignorant.   DS.

H

HABIT Habit makes an action easy until at last it becomes a necessity. **LE.**

A habit is an inner physical compulsion to go on acting as one has acted before. **A.**

HABITUS We can produce a habitus, which is not natural, but takes the place of nature, and is produced by imitation and oft repeated practice. **LE.**

HAIR Selling one's hair for gain is not altogether free from blame. **MM.** *Vide* Self-murder.

HANDMAID We may concede to theology the claim that philosophy is her handmaid. The question is whether the maid carries the torch in front of her gracious lady or the train behind her. **QuF.**

HAPPENING Everything which happens must have a cause. **CPuR.**

HAPPINESS Every one wishes to be happy. **LE.**

The greatest happiness a man can experience is to feel that he is the originator and builder of his own happiness and that what he enjoys he has acquired himself. **LE.**

No one could see to my happiness so well as I could myself.

LE.

First we must establish what happiness is. This is still a matter of controversy: some say it is found in abstinence, others in acquisition. He who has no means, but needs nothing which can be acquired by those means, appears to be happier than he who has means in plenty but needs them in plenty.

LE.

Happiness is the condition of a rational being in the world with whom everything goes according to his wish and will.

CPrR.

Happiness is the satisfaction of all our desires.   CPuR.

To be happy is necessarily the wish of every finite rational being.   CPrR.

Pure practical reason does not require that we should renounce all claim to happiness, but only that the moment duty is in question, we should take no account of happiness. It may even in certain respects be a duty to provide for happiness. But it can never be an immediate duty to promote our happiness, still less can it be the principle of all duty.   CPrR.

HAPPINESS AND MORALITY In a moral world happiness is proportioned to morality.   CPuR.

HATRED We may hate a man who has behaved hatefully and has done us an injury by publishing our secrets; he deserves hatred, but we ought not because of that to be his enemies and do him harm.   LE.

HAUGHTINESS Haughtiness feels itself superior to others and undervalues them. Haughtiness does not consist in claiming to be worth as much and to be as important as others, but in claiming an extraordinary worth and an especial importance for oneself while underestimating others. LE.

HEALTH To have a healthy mind in a healthy body is a duty to oneself. LE.

As regards health, things look unpleasant. A person may feel healthy and yet never know whether he is. QuF.

HEART The depths of the human heart are unfathomable. MM.

HELP To help others is duty, love or no love. This duty does not lose weight, because, alas! our race does not seem very lovable if we look closely at it. Yet benevolence remains a duty even towards the unlovable misanthrope. Besides, we may end by loving the persons to whom we do good. A.

HERESY Those errors that corrupt morality are termed heresy. LE.

HETERODOXY Those errors that affect theology and are corruptions of theory are called heterodoxy. LE.

HIGHEST AIM The highest aim [is] the general happiness of mankind. CPuR.

HIGHEST BEING If I try to conceive a being, as the highest reality, the question still remains, whether it exists or not. CPuR.

HIGHEST GOOD If all men were to obtain happiness without distinction of just and unjust, the highest good would not be realized, because though happiness would indeed exist, worthiness of it would not. In mankind therefore we have to look both for happiness and for merit. The combination of the two will be the highest good. LE.

HIGHEST REASON Highest reason rules according to moral laws. CPuR.

HIGHEST UNDERSTANDING The highest aim to which understanding in spiritual science is directed comprehends three objects: the freedom of the will, the immortality of the soul, and the existence of God. The interest of purely natural science in every one of these three questions is very small, and, for its sake alone, this fatiguing and ceaseless labor would hardly have been undertaken, because whatever discoveries may be made, they could never be used in the investigation of nature. . . . If, therefore, these three cardinal propositions are of no use to us, so far as natural science is concerned, their true value will probably be connected with our interest in spiritual science. CPuR.

HISTORIAN An unqualified historian does nothing but criticize the groundless assertions of others by means of his own, which are equally groundless. CPuR.

HISTORICAL COURSE The planets as seen from the earth seem also to grow now forward, now backward, and now to stand still. But if we try to take our stand on the sun, which reason only can do, they go their regular courses. QuF.

HISTORICAL KNOWLEDGE Historical knowledge is cognitio ex datis, rational knowledge cognitio ex principiis. CPuR.

HISTORY We shall discuss states and peoples, not so much referring to succession of rulers, conquests, or intrigues of states, but indicating more permanent features: produce, customs, trade, commerce, and population. IK.

HOBBY Occupation without a purpose is an occupation of leisure, a hobby; in this case we are busy only to amuse ourselves. LE.

HOLINESS The ideal of holiness is, philosophically, the most perfect in that it is the ideal of the highest pure and moral perfection; but as it is humanly unattainable it bases itself on the belief in divine aid.   LE.

HOMO Man insofar as he is a moral being cannot use himself insofar as he is a physical being as a mere means not bound to an intrinsic purpose.   MM.

Man in the system of nature is a being of slight significance and, along with other animals, considered as products of the earth, has an ordinary value. . . . But man as a person, i. e., as the subject of a morally-practical reason, is exalted above all price. For as such a one he possesses a dignity whereby he exacts the respect of all other rational beings.   MM.

HONEST An honest man cannot tell a lie, but he refrains of his own free will from telling lies.   LE.

HONESTY Were honesty not rare but a normal thing it would not be so highly regarded.   LE.

It is only in corrupt periods, in which honesty is rare.   LE.

HONOR We must distinguish between love of honor and lust for honor.   LE.

It is obviously our duty to preserve our honor, particularly in relation to the opposite sex, for whom it is a merit.   LE.

HONORING They take all their sins and lay them at God's feet, and sigh, and think thereby they honor God; they fail to see that such mean and petty eulogy from worms such as we are is but a reproach to God. They do not see that man cannot praise and eulogize God. To honor God is to obey His commandments with a willing heart, not to sing songs of praise to Him. LE.

HOPE All hoping is directed towards happiness. CPuR.

HORSE The first instrument of war among the animals was the horse for the elephant belongs to later periods. PP.

HORSERIDING Horseriding is a luxury. LE.

HOSPITALITY Hospitality signifies the right of a stranger not to be treated as an enemy when he comes to a foreign land. PP.

HOSTILITY Deceit and cunning destroy all confidence, but open hostility does not. He who openly declares himself an enemy can be relied upon. LE.

HOUSEWIFE Many a housewife has no other exercise than the scolding of her children and servants, and if they suffer it patiently, she feels a pleasant lassitude spreading through her system. A.

HUMAN BEING A human being has two standpoints from which he can regard himself: first, he finds himself subject to laws of nature; secondly, as belonging to the *intelligible world*, under moral laws which being independent from nature have their foundation not in physical experience but in free reason alone. FM. *Vide* Dualistic Philosophy.

Our statesmen say: we must take *human beings* as they are, not imagine what they ought to be. For these statesmen 'as they are' means: stubborn and inclined to rebellion, as we have made them by unjust compulsion and treacherous schemes. QuF.

HUMANE To be humane is to have sympathy with the fate

of others. Why are certain studies called *humaniora?* Because they have a refining influence upon men.   LE.

HUMANITY We must draw a distinction between the man himself and his humanity. If a man be a rogue, I disapprove of him as a man, but however wicked he is there is still some core of the goodwill in him, and if I distinguish between his humanity and the man himself I can contemplate even the rogue with pleasure.   LE.

Humanity is worthy of esteem. Even when a man is a bad man, humanity in his person is worthy of esteem. LE.

Humanity implies all essential qualities belonging to human nature, which constitute our concept of it, enlarged to a degree of complete agreement with the highest aims that would represent our idea of perfect humanity.   CPuR.

The praises of the ideal of humanity in its moral perfection lose nothing of their practical reality by counterexamples of what man now is, has been, or will be in the future.   MM.

Even though we sacrifice all life's amenities we can make up for their loss and sustain approval by maintaining the worth of our *humanity.* We may have lost everything else, and yet still retain our inherent worth.   LE.

HUMAN NATURE Human nature is very imperfect.   LE.

HUMAN QUALITIES In human nature, praiseworthy qualities never are found without concurrent variations which must run through endless shadings to the utmost imperfection.
     BS.

HUMAN RACE The ultimate destiny of the human race is the greatest moral perfection, provided that it is achieved through human freedom, whereby alone man is capable of the greatest happiness. LE.

HUMAN REASON, INSUFFICIENCY OF I have not evaded the questions by pleading the insufficiency of human reason. CPuR.

HUMBLE The speech of true reason is *humble*. LE.

HUMILITY Humility and modesty, combined with resignation, are the characteristics of such belief. The only demand it makes upon us is to do our duty to the best of our ability and for the rest to hope, without defining our hope more closely. LE.

Humility is the limitation of the high opinion we have of our moral worth by comparison of our actions with the moral law. This comparison makes us humble. LE.

The consciousness of the insignificance of one's moral worth in comparison with the law is moral humility. MM.

HYLOZOISM Hylozoism animates everything, materialism disanimates everything. DS.

HYPERCRITICISM *Hypercriticism* and subtleties are obstacles to religion: they divert from the practical. LE.

HYPOCHONDRIA Hypochondria has no definite seat in the body; the patient discovers in himself every disease he reads about in books. QuF.

HYPOCRITE We must guard against making man a hypocrite, for it is contrary to his nature to live in want and wretchedness and yet to thank God for it. How can I be grateful to God for that which I wish had not happened? LE.

HYPOTHESIS Opinion, if it is not to be utterly groundless, must be brought in connection with what is really given and therefore certain, as its ground of explanation. In that case, and in that case only, can we speak of an hypothesis.

CPuR.

I

'I AM NOT' The thought: *I am not!* is impossible, for if I am not, I cannot be conscious that I am not.   A.

IDEA I beg those who really care for philosophy to take the term idea, in its original meaning, under their special protection, so that it should no longer be lost among other expressions, by which all sorts of valuefree representations are loosely designated, to the great detriment of philosophy.
CPuR.

By idea I understand the necessary concept of reason, to which the senses can supply no corresponding object.
CPuR.

From the way in which Plato uses the term *idea*, it is easy to see that he meant by it something which was never borrowed from the senses, but flowed out from the reason.
CPuR.

IDEALISM The doctrine, which maintains a possible certainty of the objects of the external senses, is called idealism. CPuR.
Vide Idealism.

The existence of all objects of the external senses is doubtful. This uncertainty I call the ideality of external phenomena, and the doctrine of that ideality is called idealism.   CPuR.

97

Idealism assumed that the only immediate experience is the internal and that from it we can do no more than infer external things, though in an untrustworthy manner only. CPuR.

IDEALISM, EXTREME Idealism is the theory which declares the existence of objects in space, without us, as either doubtful only and not demonstrable, or as false and impossible. The former is the *problematical* idealism of Descartes, who declares one empirical assertion only to be undoubted, namely, that of I am; the latter is the *dogmatical* idealism of Berkeley, who declares space and the things in space as mere imaginations. CPuR.

IDEALIST There are two kinds of idealists, the dogmatic, who denies the existence of matter, and the sceptical, who doubts it, because he thinks it impossible to prove it. CPuR.

IDEAL OF REASON The ideal of reason must always rest on definite concepts, and serve as a rule and model, whether for imitation or for criticism. CPuR.

IDEALS We have to admit that human reason contains not only ideas, but ideals also, which have certainly practical power, and form the basis of the possible perfection of certain acts. CPuR.

Ideals, though they cannot claim reality, are not therefore to be considered as mere chimeras, but supply reason with an indispensable standard. CPuR.

IDEA OF MORALITY Without a God and without an intelligible world, the glorious ideas of morality are indeed objects of applause and admiration, but not springs of purpose and action. CPuR. *Vide* Obligation.

IDEAS, TRANSCENDENT Transcendent ideas have a merely

intelligible object, which may indeed be admitted as a transcendental object. CPuR.

IDENTITY When an object is represented to us several times, but each time with the same internal determinations, it is, so long as it is considered as an object of the pure understanding, always one and the same, one thing, not many. CPuR.

IDLENESS There are men who are occupied without a purpose; they have no serious end in view and are busy idlers, which is a silly sort of trade. LE.

In idleness we not only feel that life is fleeting but we also feel lifeless. LE.

It is self-deceit when an idler is satisfied with doing no harm. His idleness is punished by boredom; if he plays with the fine arts or with social diversions, this is called 'whiling the time away', and his boredom at least contributes towards the culture of the mind. Otherwise it is called *killing* time. A.

IGNORANCE The observations and calculations of astronomers have taught us much that is wonderful; but the most important is, that they have revealed to us the abyss of our ignorance, which otherwise human understanding could never have conceived so great. CPuR.

The consciousness of my ignorance ought, instead of forming the end of my investigations, to serve, on the contrary, as their strongest impulse. CPuR.

All ignorance is either an ignorance of things, or an ignorance of the limits of our cognition. If ignorance is accidental, it should incite us, in the former case, to investigate things dogmatically, in the latter to investigate the limits of possible knowledge critically. CPuR.

ILLEGITIMATE CHILD An illegitimate child is like contraband, it ought not to be there at all. MM.

ILLS With regard to all the ills in the world man ought to show himself steady, resolute and calm of mind. To submit to physical ills and to be the toy of accident and circumstances is contrary to the dignity of man; there is a source of strength in man's character which enables him to withstand all ills. LE.

ILLUSION Even the wisest are deceived by *illusion*. CPuR.

Illusion consists in holding the subjective ground of our judgments to be objective. PM.

What is merely illusion can never be attributed to an object as a predicate. CPuR.

Optical appearance or illusion occurs in the empirical use of the otherwise correct rules of the understanding, by which, owing to the influence of imagination, the faculty of judgment is misled. CPuR.

ILLUSTRATION Illustrations, though they may help with regard to details, often distract with regard to the whole. CPuR.
Vide Example.

IMAGE No visible *image* can be adequate to an idea of reason. CJ.

IMAGINATION Imagination is the faculty representing an object even without its presence in intuition. CPuR.

IMMANENT All principles the application of which is entirely confined within the limits of possible experience, we shall call immanent. CPuR.

IMMATERIALITY This substance, taken simply as the object of the internal sense, gives us the concept of immateriality. CPuR.

IMPERATIVES That our reason possesses legislation, is clear from the imperatives which, in all practical matters, we impose as rules on our executive powers. CPuR.

Every imperative expresses an Ought. LE.

Reason gives laws which are imperatives, that is, objective laws of freedom, and tells us what ought to take place, though perhaps it never does take place, differing therein from the laws of nature, which relate only to what does take place. CPuR.

All imperatives command either hypothetically or categorically. FM.

IMPERFECTION The very purity of the moral law bears sufficient witness to the imperfections of man; but he who seeks out the seed of evil in man is almost an advocate of the devil. LE.

IMPRESSION We see that the impressions of the senses give the first impulse to the whole faculty of knowledge. CPuR.

IMPUTATION The key to the imputation of responsibility for consequences is freedom. LE.

Imputation in the moral sense is the judgment by which someone is regarded as the author of an action, which then is called a deed and stands under laws. MM.

101

Whether a person has committed the deed with emotion or with calm deliberation, makes an important difference in imputation. MM.

Imputation clearly shows that we imagine that spiritual reason is not affected at all by the influences of the senses . . . that reason does not belong to the series of determined sensuous conditions. CPuR.

Our imputations can refer to the empirical character only. CPuR.

Action is imputed to a man's intelligible character. CPuR.

The act has to be imputed entirely to a fault. CPuR.

INCEST Incest consists in intercourse between the sexes in a form which, by reason of consanguinity, must be ruled out. LE.

Nature has implanted in our breasts a natural opposition to incest. She intended us to combine with other races and so to prevent too great a sameness in one society. Too close a connection, too intimate an acquaintance produces sexual indifference and repugnance. LE.

INCLINATION The inclinations are sources of want. FM.

Nothing can be done by force against sensual inclinations. We must outwit them. A.

All objects of the inclinations have only a conditional worth, for if the inclinations and the wants founded on them did not exist, then their object would be without value. FM.

INDIFFERENTISM Indifferentism—the mother of chaos and night in the scientific world. CPuR.

It is in vain to assume a kind of artificial indifferentism in respect to enquiries the object of which cannot be indifferent to human nature. CPuR.

INDOLENCE An indolent man avoids strife and trouble because they inconvenience him; he wants peace not from any noble and kindly motives and not because his character is gentle. LE.

INDOLENCE OF REASON We may term indolence of reason every principle which causes us to look on our investigation of nature, wherever it may be, as absolutely complete, so that reason may rest as if her task were fully accomplished. CPuR.

INEFFICIENCY Tell a man that he must be industrious and thrifty in youth, in order that he may not want in old age; this is a correct and important practical precept of the will. But it is easy to see that in this case the will is directed to something else which it is presupposed that it desires. CPrR.

INEVITABLE PROBLEMS These inevitable problems of pure understanding are God, Freedom, and Immortality. CPuR.

INFERENCE A distinction is commonly made between what is immediately known and what is only inferred. That in a figure bounded by three straight lines there are three angles, is known immediately, but that these angles together are equal to two right angles, is only inferred. CPuR.

If I place a ball on a cushion, its smooth surface is followed by a depression, while, if there is a depression in the cushion, a leaden ball does by no means follow from it. CPuR.

INFINITY We do not come nearer to the infinity, however immense a radius we assign to its activity. GTH.

A certain expansion which fills the space, for instance, heat, and every other kind of phenomenal reality, may, without leaving the smallest part of space empty, diminish by degrees in *infinitum*, and nevertheless fill space with its smaller, quite as much as another phenomenon with greater, degrees. CPuR.

INGRATITUDE Ingratitude can reach the point of hating the benefactor. MM.

INHIBITION Small inhibitions must always be interposed. A.

INJURY Injury consists in the action which violates the law; if we injure a person, that person has a right to demand from me what is requisite in accordance with the universal laws. LE.

INJUSTICE The most frequent and fertile source of human misery is not misfortune, but the injustice of man. LE.

Many people leave undone their bounden duties and yet think that they can perform those which will be accounted to them for merit. Such are the men who are guilty of much injustice in the world, who rob their fellows and then proceed to make testamentary bequests to hospitals. But a penetrating, iron voice cries out against them, and try as they may they cannot silence it by would-be meritorious acts. Such acts, indeed, aggravate their guilt, for they are like bribes. LE.

Let a man be kind and generous all his life and commit but one act of injustice to an individual, and all his acts of generosity cannot wipe out that one injustice. LE.

INNER VOICE It is as if man heard an inner voice saying that there must be some moral background to the earthly life, even though concerning its nature a good deal of nonsense was hatched out. CJ.

INNOCENCE Innocence is indeed a glorious thing, only, on the other hand, it is very sad that it cannot well maintain itself, and is easily seduced. FM.

We are innocent of moral transgressions only if our dispositions are pure. If his dispositions are not pure, man is judged before the court of justice of morality as if he had actually committed the offenses. LE.

INNOVATION Few only have that pliability of intellect to take in the whole of a system, if it is new; still fewer have an inclination for it, because they dislike every innovation. CPuR.

INSINCERITY Insincerity is merely want of candor in confessing before one's inner judge. MM.

Insincerity is a lack of scrupulosity which leads to wishful thinking. A lover wishing to find nothing but good in his beloved may make himself blind to her obvious defects. MM.

INSTRUCTION Instruction will have to take the same path. The teacher should mould first an intelligent man, then a reasoning man, and finally a scholar. IK.

The method of instruction suitable for philosophy is zetetic, that is, exploratory. Only when the understanding is already somewhat trained, can it become dogmatic, i.e., assertive. IK.

INTELLECT The understanding would not be wronged in the

least, if we assumed that some being does not rest on empirical conditions, but on mere grounds of the intellect. CPuR.

INTELLIGENCE Intelligence is the faculty of a subject by which it is able to represent to itself what by its quality cannot enter the senses. DFP.

I exist as such an intelligence, which is simply conscious of its power of connection. CPuR.

INTELLIGENT BEING It must be admitted that we cannot represent to ourselves another intelligent being without putting ourselves in its place with that formula of our consciousness. CPuR.

INTELLIGIBLE Whatever in an object of the senses is not itself phenomenal, I call intelligible. CPuR.

An intelligible, that is, a moral world. CPuR.

INTELLIGIBLE CAUSE *Vide* Moral Ground.

INTELLIGIBLE GROUND This intelligible ground does not touch the empirical questions, but concerns only the thought in the pure understanding of the reason. CPuR. *Vide* Ground, Intelligible.

INTELLIGIBLE OBJECT The conditioned existence of all natural phenomena, not being founded in itself, requires us to look out for something different from all phenomena, that is, for an intelligible object in which there should be no more. CPuR.

INTELLIGIBILIA If I admit things which are objects of the understanding only, such things would be called intelligibilia. CPuR. *Vide* Noumenon.

INTEMPERANCE Intemperance is a sign of lack of taste.   LE.

INTENTION Nobody could explain the production of even a blade of grass by laws without any intention.   CJ.
Vide Grass.

INTERFERENCE Nothing but mischief must arise from any foreign interference or any attempt to direct reason, against her own natural inclination, towards objects forced upon her from without.   CPuR.

INTERNATIONAL LAW The idea of international law presumes the separate existence of many independent states.
PP.

INTERVENTION, FOREIGN No state shall by force interfere with the constitution or government of another state.   PP.

INTIMACY There can be perfect and complete intimacy only in matters of disposition and sentiment, but we have certain natural frailties which ought to be concealed for the sake of decency, lest humanity be outraged. Even to our best friend we must not reveal ourselves, in our natural state as we know it ourselves. To do so would be loathsome. LE.

Too intimate an acquaintance produces sexual indifference.
LE.

INTOLERANCE The man who cannot contemplate the imperfections of others without hatred is intolerant. We often meet men who are intolerant of the views of others from personal dislike; their intolerance makes them intolerable and they get themselves disliked in turn.   LE.

INTOXICATION All dumb intoxication that does not animate social conversation is discreditable.   A.

To guess the true temperament or character of a person while he is drunk is futile, because the liquid circulating in his blood stream changes him completely.   A.

INTROSPECTION We may treat our body as we please, provided our motives are those of self-preservation.   LE.

We keep ourselves under observation not by eavesdropping but by watchful attention to our actions. The effort to know ourselves and so to discover whether we are good or bad must be made in the practical business of living.   LE.

Self-observation is impossible during emotion and useless when the mainsprings of action are at rest.   A.

INTROVERSION The propensity of introversion with all its deceptions can only be cured by a return to the external world.   A.

INTUITION Whatever the process and the means may be by which knowledge reaches its objects, there is one that reaches them directly, and forms the ultimate material of all thought, viz., intuition.   CPuR.

INTUITION, EMPIRICAL All concepts refer to empirical intuitions, that is, to data of a possible experience.   CPuR.

An intuition of an object, by means of sensation, is called empirical.   CPuR.

INVERSION I cannot invert the order, and place that which happens before that on which it follows.   CPuR.

INVESTIGATION Freedom of investigation is the best means to consolidate the truth.   LE.

The investigation of nature pursues its own course, guided

by the chain of natural causes only, according to general
laws.   CPuR.

I THINK The *I think* expresses the act of determining my own
spiritual existence.   CPuR.

J

JEALOUSY When a man compares himself with another and finds that the other has many more good points, he becomes jealous of each and every good point he discovers in the other, and tries to depreciate it so that his own good points may stand out.   LE.

Many businessmen are jealous of each other; so are many scholars, particularly in the same line of scholarship; and women are liable to be jealous of each other regarding men.   LE.

The jealousy of emulations is more difficult than the jealousy of grudge and so is much the less frequent of the two.
LE.

JOB In the sacred book Job says to his friends: 'Will you defend God with wrong?' The divine judgment favored the honest man and condemned the religious flatterers. His morality was not the result of his faith, but his faith was the result of his morality. He did not base his religion on currying favor with God but on a good life.
> The Failure of all Philosophical Attempts
> Towards a Theodicy.

JOKE Jokes mostly consist in arousing expectations which are suddenly brought to a stop; we then react to the relaxation by a vibration of the bodily organs.   CJ.

111

JOURNEY Miles near to town seem shorter than those farther away; for as we proceed on our way our attention is diverted by many objects near town, but farther away there is nothing to see and the miles seem long. But if at the end of the journey we look back, the journey seems to have been short, because, except for a short length of it near to town, there was nothing to notice and to remember. LE.

JOY To feel and enjoy one's life is to be continuously driven out of one's present condition. A.

JUDGE The inner judge is thought of as another person. MM.
Vide Self-obligation.

> The judge within us is just. He takes the action for what it is and makes no allowance for human defectiveness, if only we have the will to listen for his voice and do not stifle it. LE.

> The judge must either condemn or acquit, not merely form a judgment. LE.

> A benevolent judge is unthinkable. A judge must be just; a ruler can be benevolent. LE.

JUDGES As impartial judges we must take no account of whether it be the good or the bad cause which the two champions defend. It is best to let them fight it out between themselves in the hope that, after they have rather tired out than injured each other, they may themselves perceive the uselessness of their quarrel, and part as good friends. CPuR.

JUDGMENT We associate Judgment with the feeling of aesthetic pleasure. CJ.

> Flowers, many birds and sea-shells show free beauty without regard to their purpose. So do ornaments or musical rhapsodies. But the beauty of a human being or of a horse

or church is judged also by what its purpose is. Here we speak of adherent beauty; the aesthetic judgment is then no longer pure. CJ.

Much is gained if we are able to bring a number of investigations under the formula of one single problem. For we thus not only facilitate our own work by defining it accurately, but enable also everybody else who likes to examine it to form a *judgment*, whether we have really done justice to our purpose or not. CPuR.

JUDGMENT, LOGICAL A judgment may be false or groundless though in itself it is free from all contradictions. CPuR.

A judgment is a mediate knowledge of an object, or a representation of a representation of it. CPuR.

JUDGMENT, MORAL We see that, in judging of voluntary actions, we can get only so far as the intelligible ground, but not beyond. We can see that reason is causally free, that it determines, independent of sensibility, and therefore is capable of being the sensuously unconditioned condition. CPuR.

JUDGMENT OF TASTE The satisfaction felt in a judgment of taste is free from all interest; i. e., the object as such brings no advantage and arouses no desire. CJ.

JURISPRUDENCE Jurisprudence is not concerned with the discharge of obligations from duty, but from compulsion; it considers them in their relation to compulsion, and stresses the sanctions of compulsion. LE.

JURIST Jurists, when speaking of rights and claims, distinguish in every lawsuit the question of right from the question of fact. CPuR.

113

JURY In England butchers and doctors do not sit on a jury because they are accustomed to the sight of death and hardened. LE.

JUSTICE If justice perishes, human life on earth would no longer have any value. MM.

Justice must not throw herself away at any price. MM.

My expectation of remuneration is a demand for the payment of a debt. We can have no claim for payment against God. LE.

K

KANT DUTY-BOUND Duty! Thou sublime and mighty name that dost embrace nothing charming or insinuating, but requirest submission, and yet seekest not to move the will by threatening aught that would arouse natural aversion or terror, but merely holdest forth a law which of itself finds entrance into the mind, and yet gains reluctant reverence, a law before which all inclinations are dumb, even though they secretly counter-work it.   CPrR.

KANT'S ACHIEVEMENT After having discovered the reason of—and consequently the mode of removing—the doubts and contradictions into which the understanding fell, I have solved them to its perfect satisfaction.   CPuR.

KANT'S BIRTHPLACE A large town such as Koenigsberg on the Pregel River, centre of a district, containing government offices and a university, suitably situated for overseas trade and for intercourse with adjoining as well as remoter countries of different languages and customs—such a town is the right place for gaining knowledge concerning men and the world even without traveling.   A.
Vide Traveling.

KANT'S BREATHING A few years ago I was plagued now and then by a nasal catarrh and cough, particularly inconvenient when I was going to bed. Indignant about this disturbance of my nightly sleep, I resolved to keep my lips firmly closed and draw air through the nose. I succeeded

115

finally in drawing a strong current of air through the nose, whereupon I fell immediately asleep.   QuF.

KANT'S COURAGE I feel the full force of the obstacles facing me, and yet I do not lose heart. Guided by a slight conjecture, I have ventured on a dangerous voyage and already I see the promontories of the new land.   GTH.

KANT'S DEMOCRATIC CONVICTION I have learned to respect human nature, and I should deem myself far more useless than the ordinary working man if I did not believe that this consideration could give worth to all others to establish the rights of man.   BS.

KANT'S DETACHMENT How many things there are which I do not need!   DS.

KANT'S DISTRACTION In every lecture I first announce what I am going to say, show the object towards which I proceed and point back to the starting-point. But now it happens to me that when I try to connect the last thought with the first, I must suddenly ask my listeners, Where was I? From where did I start?, and this is not from a defect of mind or memory. It is involuntary distraction.   QuF.

KANT'S FATHER My father suffered considerably; nevertheless, even in conversation amongst his own family he spoke about this quarrel with such forbearance and love towards his opponents, that although I was then only a boy, I shall never forget it.   IK.

KANT'S HUMILITY The starry view of a countless multitude of heavenly bodies annihilates as it were my importance as an animal creature, which after it has been for a short time provided with vital power, one knows not how, must again give back the matter of which it was formed to the planet it inhabits.   CPrR.

KANT'S MENTAL DEBILITY I make no secret of the debility of my mind and avow that usually I understand least what everybody else understands quite easily. So, on account of my impotence, I claim to be assisted by those brilliant minds. May their wisdom fill the gaps which my defective insight had to leave open.
Attempt at Introducing Negative Quantities into Philosophy.

KANT'S MORAL FIBRE I have not to search for the moral law and conjecture it as though it were veiled in darkness or were in the transcendent region beyond my horizon; I see it before me and connect it directly with the consciousness of my existence.   CPrR.

KANT'S MOTHER I shall never forget my mother, for she planted and fostered the first germ of good in me; she opened my heart to the impressions of nature, she awoke and enlarged my thoughts, and her teaching has always had an enduring and wholesome influence in my life.   IK.

KANT'S PAINS When I suffer from sleepless fits, I turn my thoughts with great exertion to some indifferent object selected by me, no matter what. It might be the name of Cicero and how many ideas or images are associated with it. When I thus turn my attention away from unpleasant sensations, they soon become blunted and sleepiness gets the better of them. My pains are certainly not merely imagined, for in the morning I may find the toes of my left foot glowing red.   QuF.

KANT'S PARENTS They possessed the highest that man can possess—that calm, that serenity, that inward peace which is not disturbed by any passion. No trouble, no persecution dismayed them; no contest had the power to stir them up to anger or hostility.   IK.

KANT'S PASSION FOR KNOWLEDGE I am myself by inclina-

117

tion a searcher after truth. I feel a consuming thirst for knowledge, a restless passion to advance in it as well as a profound satisfaction in every forward step.   BS.

KANT'S RETROSPECT According to the Bible our life lasts seventy years, and if very long, fourscore years, and though it was pleasant, it has been labor and sorrow.   IK.

KANT'S SELF-DEFENSE I am often accused of obscurity, perhaps even of intentional vagueness in my philosophical discourse which gives itself the air of deep insight.   MM.

KANT'S SERENITY I do not fear to die. I assure you, as in the presence of God, that if on this very night, suddenly the summons to death were to reach me, I should bear it with calmness, should raise my hands to heaven and say, "Blessed be God!"   IK.

KANT'S SHREWDNESS I live among those who know how to pretend, and I flatter myself I possess some shrewdness too.   DH.

KANT'S SWEETHEART To be in love with metaphysics is my fate, although I can hardly boast of favors received from her.   DS.

KANT'S THIRST Sometimes when I feel very thirsty at night I breathe in repeatedly and *drink* air through the nose, whereupon my thirst is completely quenched within a few seconds. This thirst is a morbid stimulus which can be canceled out by a counter-stimulus.   QuF.

KANT'S THOROUGHNESS My chief aim in this work has been thoroughness; and I make bold to say, that there is not a single metaphysical problem that does not find its solution, or at least the key to its solution, here.   CPuR.

KANT'S UNANSWERED QUESTIONS Why do I refuse to make room for the aspiring young generation? Why do I cut off the usual enjoyments of life simply to live longer? Why do I protract a feeble life to unusual length by privations? Why do I upset the yearly mortality rate? Why do I subject to my own firm resolution what was formerly called fate, to which people submitted humbly? QuF.

KANT'S WALKS Strenuous thinking during a walk tires one quickly, whereas if accompanied by a free fanciful play of the imagination the bodily motion is relaxing. QuF.

KILLING If a man kills another in a fit of jealous temper his deed is not as evil as that of a man who in cold blood and of malice prepense encompasses the death of another. LE.

KINDHEARTED Men pride themselves that they have a kind heart because they wish that every one might be happy; but merely to wish is not the sign of a kind heart; we are kindhearted only in so far as we actually contribute to the happiness of others: that alone betokens a kind heart. LE.

KINDNESS A kindly heart gets more pleasure and satisfaction from doing good to others than from its own enjoyment of the good things of life; the inclination to do good is a necessity to it, which must be satisfied. LE.

KINGDOM OF GOD The highest possible perfection of human nature—this is the kingdom of God on earth. LE.

KNOWLEDGE Objects which affect our senses, rouse the activity of our understanding to convert the raw material of our sensuous impressions into a *knowledge* of objects. CPuR.

Under the sway of understanding our knowledge must not remain a rhapsody, but must become a system, because thus alone can the essential objects of understanding be supported and advanced. By system I mean the unity of various kinds of *knowledge* under one idea.   CPuR.

God created the world for knowledge.   LE.

Plato knew very well that our faculty of knowledge was filled with a much higher craving than merely to spell out natural phenomena. He knew that our understanding, if left to itself, tries to soar up to knowledge to which no object sensuous experience may give can ever correspond; but which nevertheless is real, and by no means a mere cobweb of the brain.   CPuR.

All human knowledge begins with intuitions, advances to concepts, and ends with ideas.   CPuR.

Our *knowledge* of the world has two sources: the intellect and the senses.   FP.

There would be no excuse, if reason were to surrender a *causality* which it knows, and have recourse to obscure and indemonstrable principles of explanation, which it does not know.   CPuR.

All knowledge has two ends by which it can be grasped: one a priori, the other a posteriori.   DS.

I shall define theoretical *knowledge* as one by which I know what there is, practical knowledge as one by which I represent to myself what ought to be. Hence the theoretical use of reason is that by which I know that something is, while the practical use of reason is that by which I know what ought to be.   CPuR.

KNOWLEDGE, ADVANCEMENT OF What can be more mischievous to the advancement of knowledge than to communicate even our thoughts in a falsified form, to conceal doubts which we feel in our own assertions, and to impart an appearance of conclusiveness to arguments which we know ourselves to be inconclusive?   CPuR.

KNOWLEDGE, ELEMENTS OF Intuition and concepts constitute the elements of all our knowledge, so that neither concepts without an intuition corresponding to them, nor intuition without concepts can yield any real knowledge.
CPuR.

KNOWLEDGE, HUMAN There are two roots of human knowledge, viz., sensibility and the understanding, objects being given by the former and thought by the latter.   CPuR.

KNOWLEDGE, KINDS OF There must be a kind of knowledge in which there is no sensibility, representing spiritual values, while through the empirical use of our understanding we know natural phenomena. Hence it would seem to follow that, beside the empirical use of the categories, there was another one, pure and yet objectively valid. Here, in fact, quite a new field would seem to be open, a world, as it were, realized in thought only, which would be a more, and not a less, worthy object for the pure understanding. CPuR.

KNOWLEDGE, PURE Knowledge, if mixed up with nothing empirical, is called pure.   CPuR.

L

LAMENTATION Whining and lamentation are as useless in foro divino as they are in foro humano. LE.

LANGUAGE In spite of the great wealth of our languages, a thoughtful mind is often at a loss for an expression that should square exactly with its concept; and for want of which he cannot make himself altogether intelligible, either to others or to himself. To coin new words is to arrogate to oneself legislative power in matters of language. It is always advisable to look about, in dead and learned languages, whether they do not contain such a concept and its adequate expression. Even if it should happen that the original meaning of the word had become somewhat uncertain, it is better nevertheless to determine and fix the meaning which principally belonged to it, than to spoil our labor by becoming unintelligible. CPuR.

LATIN I have to apologize for the many Latin expressions which, contrary to good taste, have crept in instead of their native equivalents. My only excuse is, that I thought it better to sacrifice something of the elegance of language, rather than to throw any impediments in the way of real students, by the use of inaccurate and obscure expressions. CPuR.

LAUGHING Laughing is masculine. A.

LAW When a lawyer knows law historically only, he is rendered

very unfit for a good judge, and utterly so for a legislator.
Logic.

Rules so far as they are objective, are called laws. CPuR.
Vide Rule.

Particular laws of nature are subject to more general laws.
CPuR.

LAW, HUMAN The law should be so sacred and inviolable that it is a crime to doubt it; therefore, it is represented as derived from a divine legislator. **MM.**

LAWGIVER A man who propounds that a law which is in accordance with his will shall be binding on others, promulgates a law, and is a lawgiver. **LE.**

LAW, INTERNATIONAL To establish right in war is the most difficult part of *international law*. How introduce a law in this lawless state without contradicting oneself? **MM.**

LAWS OF NATURE Reason is always present, while *laws of nature* must usually be sought with labor. **PM.**

LAWYER A lawyer might use deceptive arguments in order to exploit to his advantage the unwariness of his opponent.
CPuR.

Lawyers must regard the preservation of life as the highest duty, because the threat of death is their most powerful weapon in examining a man. **LE.**

LAW OF MORALITY The law which has no other motive but to *deserve* to be happy, I call moral. It dictates how we ought to conduct ourselves in order to deserve happiness.
CPuR.

LAW OF NATURE Even laws of nature carry with them a character of necessity, and thus lead to the supposition that they rest on grounds which are valid before all experience. CPuR.

The law of nature, that everything which happens has a cause . . . is a law of the understanding, which can on no account be surrendered, and from which no single natural phenomenon can be exempted. CPuR.

LAWSUIT We considered it advisable to write down the records of this lawsuit in full detail, and to deposit them in the archives of human reason. CPuR.

LAZINESS Laziness reduces the degree of life. LE.

Nature has wisely endowed some men with laziness, as otherwise their malice would be even more harmful. A.

LEAGUE OF NATIONS A league of nations would not have to be a state consisting of nations. PP.

LEARNING The student should not learn thoughts but should learn how to think. He should not be carried but guided, so that in the future he will be capable of walking by himself. So now he expects he will learn philosophy. But that is impossible. What he must learn is how to philosophize. IK.

Wide learning ennobles man, and the love of study stifles many a base inclination within us. LE.

LEGAL CONSTRAINT The constraint of law alone limits our freedom in such a way that it may consist with the freedom of others and with the common good. CPuR.

LEGALITY The mere conformity or nonconformity of an action with the law, without regard to the incentive of the action, is called legality; but when the idea of duty arising from the law is at the same time the incentive of the action, then the conformity is called its morality.   MM.

LEGISLATION The more legislation and government are in harmony with that idea, the rarer, no doubt, punishments would become.   CPuR.

It is an old desideratum, which at some time, however distant, may be realized, that, instead of the endless variety of civil laws, their principles might be discovered, for thus alone the secret might be found of what is called simplifying legislation.   CPuR.

LETTER If I am left alone in a room and I see a letter lying open on the table, it would be contemptible to try to read it; a right-thinking man would not do so.   LE.

LEWDNESS The vice engendered by carnal lust is called lewdness.   MM.

LIAR A liar, even though by his lies he does no harm to any one, yet becomes an object of contempt, he throws away his personality; his behavior is vile, he has transgressed his duty towards himself.   LE.

LIBERTY The unconditioned is called liberty.   CPuR.
                Vide Freedom.

LIBIDO, VAGA This way of satisfying sexuality is vaga libido, in which one satisfies the inclinations of others for gain. It is possible for either sex.   LE.

LIE Every lie is objectionable and contemptible in that we purposely let people think that we are telling them our thoughts and do not do so.   LE.

126

A child which tells a *lie* should not be punished, but shamed: it should feel ashamed, contemptible, nauseated as though it had been bespattered with dirt. If, however, he is punished instead—say, at school—he thinks to himself that once out of school he runs no risk of being punished and he will also try by tricks to escape punishment. LE.

LIES, DETESTABLE Nations had a right idea of their duties, and were aware that lies were detestable, without having the proper concept of God. LE.

LIFE Life consists in the union of soul and body. LE.

He who has no inner worth sets greater store by his life, but he who has a greater inner worth places a lesser value upon his life. LE.

Life is short and all happiness fleeting. LE.

It is quite natural that every one of us should have a greater appreciation of our *present* life, which we can know and feel more clearly. LE.

There is no material benefit in life so great that we should regard it as a duty to risk our life for it. LE.

If we have done nothing in life except waste our time and we review in retrospect the span of our life, we are puzzled to know how it has passed so quickly; we have done so little in it. LE.

Life is not to be highly regarded for its own sake. I should endeavor to preserve my own life only so far as I am worthy to live. LE.

Whatever in the world contains a principle of life, can hardly be material.   DS.

LIMIT Every limit of extension is in space.   CPuR.

LIMITING As on the one side we limit understanding lest it should lose the thread of the empirical condition and lose itself in transcendent explanations incapable of being represented in concreto, thus, on the other side, we want to limit the law of the purely empirical use of the understanding, lest it should venture to decide on the possibility of things in general, and declare the intelligible ideas or moral grounds to be impossible, because it has been shown to be useless for the explanation of natural phenomena.
CPuR.

LITERATI From the scholars proper we must distinguish the *literati* who, as instruments of the government, are invested by it with an office, not always to the benefit of the sciences.
QuF.

LOGIC That logic has followed that secure scientific method, may be seen from the fact that since Aristotle it has not had to retrace a single step, unless we choose to consider as improvements the removal of some unnecessary subtleties, or the clearer definition of its matter, both of which refer to the elegance rather than to the solidity of the science.
CPuR.

Some logicians presuppose psychological principles in logic. But to introduce such principles into logic, is absurd. In logic understanding is concerned with itself alone.   CPuR.

The limits of logic are definitely fixed by the fact, that it is a science which has nothing to do but fully to exhibit and strictly to prove all formal rules of thought.   CPuR.

Common logic gives an instance how all the simple acts of understanding can be enumerated completely and systematically. CPuR.

LOGICAL PARALOGISM The logical paralogism consists in the formal faultiness of a conclusion, without any reference to its contents. CPuR.

LOGICAL PRINCIPLE A purely logical principle takes no account of any of the contents of our knowledge, and looks only to its logical form. CPuR.

LOQUACIOUSNESS Loquaciousness in men is contemptible and contrary to the strength of the male. LE.

LOTTERY Many people think to themselves that they would do this or that magnanimous action if they won a substantial prize in a lottery, and if perchance they do win it, nothing comes of their good intentions. So it is with the evildoer who, faced with death, is full of honorable and upright dispositions. LE.

LOVE We say that a man loves someone when he has an inclination towards another person. If by this love we mean true human love, then it admits of no distinction between types of persons, or between young and old. But a love that springs merely from sexual impulse cannot be love at all, but only appetite. Human love is goodwill, affection, promoting the happiness of others and finding joy in their happiness. But it is clear that, when a person loves another purely from sexual desire, none of these factors enter into the love. LE.

We can also love a bad man without in the least respecting him. LE.

Reason taught them that the sexual stimulus can be intensified by imagination and that the inclination can be made more permanent. Refusal led them from mere animal-urge to *love*.

Preamble Beginning of the History of Mankind.

There are two kinds of love, the love of good-will and the love of good-pleasure. The love of good-will consists in the wish and inclination to promote the happiness of others, the love of good-pleasure in the satisfaction which we ourselves derive from appreciating the perfections of another.   LE.

Our inclinations to love and wish for their happiness should not be sentimental longings. Such ineffectual cravings we should seek to avoid, and cherish only practical desires. LE.

The greatest love I can have for another is to love him as myself. I cannot love another more than I love myself. But if I am to love him as I love myself, I must be sure that he will love me as he loves himself.   LE.

LOVE OF GOD To love God is to do as He commands with a willing heart.   LE.

LUST A lust is called unnatural when a man is aroused not by a real object but by imagining it, thus creating it himself unpurposively.   MM.

Sexual love is destined for the preservation of the species. Is it permissible for a man to use his sex organs merely to satisfy his animal *lust*? This idea is revolting to such a degree that even to mention this vice is thought immoral.   MM.

Lust and laziness must not merely be guided but dominated.   LE.

LUXURY We may call excess of pleasure and amusement luxury. Where luxury prevails, suicide is usually common.   LE.

Luxury is indirectly an infringement of morality. On the other hand, it promotes the arts and the sciences and develops man's talents; it thus seems to be the condition for which humanity is designed. It refines morality.   LE.

Luxury requires good taste, and is found only with people who possess that quality; by its variety it clarifies man's judgment, gives occupation to many people and vitalizes the entire social structure.   LE.

M

MACHINE AND ORGANISM A machine has merely motive-power, but an organism has formative power. It has reproductive power which cannot be explained mechanically.
CJ.

MADNESS People say often, 'he has become mad from love, or from having studied too much, or from pride', but such factors can never be the cause of madness though possibly its effects. As for young people studying too much, there is certainly no such danger.
A.

MAGNANIMITY Magnanimity and kidness are meritorious; we cannot expect every one to be kind and generous, and men who show these qualities are highly esteemed and honored.
LE.

MAGNIFYING Telescope and microscope only magnify what is constantly before us, unnoticed, unseen.
A.

MAGNITUDE The magnitude is the determination which can only be thought by a judgment possessing quantity. CPuR.

MALICE The treachery of secret malice, if it became universal, would mean the end of all confidence.
LE.

MAN To ask, 'Why does man exist?' is a meaningless question.
LE.

Man is his own ultimate purpose and the true aim of all culture.
A.

Nature does not make the slightest exception in favor of man but treats him like any other animal. CJ.

Man is a being intended for society. MM.

Experience seems to confirm that man is a mean between the two extremes of good and bad. RR.

Man is forced to be a good citizen even if not a good person. PP.

We can judge the heart of man by his treatment of animals. LE.

Men prefer the easier course. LE.

Man is not a thing, not a beast. LE.

A man of inner worth does not shrink from death; he would die rather than live as object of contempt, a member of a gang of scoundrels in the galleys; but the worthless man prefers the galleys, almost as if they were his proper place. LE.

Man is free to dispose of his condition but not of his person; he himself is an end and not a means; all else in the world is of value only as a means, but man is a person and not a thing and therefore not a means. It is true that a person can serve as a means for others, but only in a way whereby he does not cease to be a person and an end. LE.

We sometimes meet men whose faces show them to be incorrigible rogues. On the other hand, an honest and upright man cannot become vicious. LE.

No man shall be used as a means for another's intentions and treated as a thing. **MM.**

Man is to himself partly a natural phenomenon, partly, however, namely with reference to certain faculties, a purely intelligible object, because the actions of these faculties cannot be ascribed to the receptivity of sensibility. We call these spiritual and causefree faculties understanding and reason. It is the latter, in particular, which is entirely distinguished from all empirically conditioned forces or faculties. **CPuR.**

MANHOOD If a man for gain or profit submits to all indignities and makes himself the plaything of another, he casts away the worth of his manhood. **LE.**

MANIFOLD, THE The manifold is given us in a sensuous intuition. **CPuR.**

MANKIND Mankind is not rich in principles. **LE.**

MARITAL PLEASURE A young bachelor feels vexed that he must forego the pleasures of the married man; but though the married man has the same appetite he can forego gratifying it more easily, knowing that he can gratify it whenever he will. **LE.**

MARRIAGE A suitor might make a profitable marriage if only he could disregard a wart on the face or a gap in the teeth of his beloved. But it is a malicious trick of our mind to be influenced by such defects. **A.**

A man may act kindly towards his wife from love, but if his inclination has evaporated he ought to do so from obligation. **LE.** *Vide* Union.

The sole condition on which we are free to make use of

our sexual desire depends upon the right to dispose over the person as a whole—over the welfare and happiness and generally over all the circumstances of that person. But how am I to obtain these rights over the whole person? Only by giving that person the same rights over the whole of myself. This happens only in *marriage*. LE.

MATHEMATICAL The work of understanding by means of the construction of concepts is called mathematical. CPuR.

MATHEMATICS Mathematical propositions do not require examples. An example in such a case is no part of the proof; it merely serves as an illustration. LE.

Mathematics has followed the safe way of a science. CPuR.

The science of mathematics presents the most brilliant example of how pure understanding may successfully enlarge its domain without the aid of experience. CPuR.

MATRIMONY Matrimony is an agreement between two persons by which they grant each other reciprocal rights, each of them undertaking to surrender the whole of their person to the other with a complete right of disposal over it. LE.

Matrimony is the only condition in which use can be made of one's sexuality. LE.

MATTER Substance appearing in space, we call matter. CPuR.

In a natural phenomenon I call that which corresponds to the sensation its matter. CPuR.

Matter is not adequate to the idea of a necessary spiritual Being. CPuR.

We can say: 'Give me matter and I will build a world
out of it.'   GTH.

MAXIMS Practical laws, in so far as they become at the same
time subjective grounds of actions, that is, subjective prin-
ciples, are called maxims.   CPuR.

Philosophy becomes aware of the different meanings in
the same word.   CPrR.

MEANS AND END Whoever wills the end, wills also the means
in his power which are indispensably necessary thereto.
                                                                                                     FM.

MECHANISM According to the idea of a mechanism [we] explain the mutual chemical workings of matter.   CPuR.

MECHANISM AND REASON The mechanism of nature refers
to the subject in so far as it is a natural phenomenon, but
the subject as a spiritual and moral being does not stand
under the conditions of time being determined solely by the
moral laws of timeless or unmechanical reason.   CPrR.

MEDICAL PHYSIOLOGY Medical physiology enlarges its very
limited empirical knowledge of the purposes of the members of an organic body by a principle inspired by pure
reason only.   CPuR.

MEDICAL PRACTICE Medical practice is philosophical if it
governs the way of life through the power of the mind
and self-imposed discipline. It is mechanical if it relies
on the chemist and the surgeon.   QuF.

MELANCHOLY Having tasted the refinements of pleasure, and
being deprived of them, they give way to grief, sorrow,
and melancholy.   LE.

137

MEMORY When a man hopes that after he is dead his memory shall be respected and honored by those he leaves behind, his impulse to honor clearly does not involve self-interest. Apart from such honor no one would devote himself to the pursuit of knowledge.   LE.

There is a technique for memorizing words which mostly, instead of relieving the mind, adds an additional burden. A.

MERCHANT The merchant wants to be considered rich because it is useful to him.   LE.

MERCY To exercise charity from pity is called mercy, an insulting kind of benefaction bestowed on the unworthy. This kind of doing good ought not to occur at all.   MM.
Vide Sexual Love.

MERIT Whatever has value we can prize, but we can only prefer in honor that which has the value of merit.   LE.

The greater the fight a man puts up against his natural inclinations the more it is to be imputed to him for merit.
LE.

METAPHYSICIAN The worker in pure philosophy, logic, or metaphysics, must keep his object floating before his mind and present the whole system at once. So it is not surprising if the metaphysician becomes, earlier than other scholars, an invalid.   QuF.

METAPHYSIC OF MORALS Just as the metaphysic of nature can be applied to the objects of experience, so the metaphysic of morals can be applied to the empirical nature of man.   MM.

METAPHYSICS There arises the idea of a twofold metaphysics, a metaphysics of nature and a metaphysics of morals.   FM.

138

How much metaphysics may disgust those alleged teachers of wisdom, it still is an indispensable duty for those who oppose metaphysics to go back to its principles, and to begin by going to school. MM.

There was a time when Metaphysics held a royal place among all sciences. At present it is the fashion to despise Metaphysics, and the poor matron, forlorn and forsaken, complains like Hecuba. CPuR.

That the human mind will ever give up metaphysical researches entirely, is as little to be expected, as that we should prefer to give up breathing altogether, to avoid inhaling impure air. PM.

It is the battle-field of those endless controversies which is called Metaphysics. CPuR.

Metaphysics is a completely isolated and speculative science which declines all teaching of experience, and rests on concepts only. CPuR.

Metaphysics has for the real object of its investigations three ideas only, God, Freedom, and Immortality. CPuR.

MIND The mind must ensure that it establishes an autocracy over the body so that the latter cannot change the mind's condition. LE.

On the vast map of the mind, obviously a few points only are illuminated, the rest is darkness. A.

MIRACLE Reasonable men, even though in theory they believe in miracles, never tolerate them in practical business. . . . A judge may believe in miracles when in church, but if a delinquent tells him that the devil has tempted him, he will not listen, for he cannot summon the devil as a witness. RR.

139

MISANTHROPY Misanthropy is hatred of mankind and may arise from either of two sources, shyness or enmity. In the first case, the misanthrope is afraid of men, deeming them all his enemies; in the second, he is himself the enemy of others.　　　　　　　　　　　　　　　　　　　LE.

MISDEED Often the weakness which dissuades a man from the committing of a misdeed is mistaken by him as virtue.　MM.

MISER A miser will forgo a small advantage in order to gain a greater, but will do so with reluctance because he would rather gain both advantages.　　　　　　　　　　　　LE.

A wealthy miser who entertains once in a while piles up the food on his guests' plates, but gives no thought to variety.　　　　　　　　　　　　　　　　　　　　LE.

The rich miser feeds himself on the thought of pleasure, knowing that it is within his reach. He is fashionably dressed, drives about in state, eats twelve-course dinners every day, but all in thought; for if he wished to he could do all this at any time. The very possession of wealth enables him both to enjoy and to forego all pleasures.　　　　　　　　　　　　　　　　LE. *Vide* Elderly.

Misers are also as a rule very devout. As they have no amusement and do not entertain socially, because it all costs money, their mind is occupied with anxious thoughts. They want comfort and support in their anxiety and look to God for it, by means of a fanatical devoutness, which, after all, costs nothing.　　　　　　　　　　　　　　　LE.

MISERLY As regards sex, women are more inclined to be miserly than men. This is in keeping with the nature of woman, for the women have to be more sparing since they are spending money which they do not earn themselves. The man, who earns the money, is in a position to be the more generous. LE.

MISERY I see a man miserable and I feel for him; but it is useless to wish that he might be rid of his misery; I ought to try to rid him of it. LE.

MISFORTUNE Misfortune and ills should be regarded with displeasure, not as such, but only if they are caused by man. LE.

We shudder at the thought of some great misfortune, but when it befalls us we find it bearable. LE.

If every one in the town had nothing but bread and water for food and drink, I should be satisfied with so simple a diet and would submit to it with a cheerful mind; but if every one else were able to enjoy sumptuous repasts and I alone had to live in a wretched state, I should feel unhappy and regard it as a misfortune. LE.

MISOLOGY Misology is hatred of reason. FM.

MOB If you raise the cry of high treason, and call together the ignorant mob as it were to extinguish a conflagration—you simply render yourself ridiculous. CPuR.

MOCKER The mocker is no respecter of company or occasion. LE.

MODALITY The principles of modality are nothing but explanations of the concepts of possibility, reality, and necessity, in their empirical employment. CPuR.

The real does conceptually not contain more than the possible. CPuR. *Vide* Reality and Possibility.

141

MODESTY Moderation in claims generally, i.e., voluntary restriction of one's self-love in regard to the self-love of others, is called modesty. MM.

MOHAMMEDANISM Mohammedanism has chosen badly by permitting opium and forbidding wine. MM.

MOMENTUM The degree of the reality as a cause we call a momentum, for instance, the momentum of gravity. CPuR.

MONARCHY A monarchy should be ruled in the spirit of a republic. QuF.

MONEY Money enables a man to bring others under his power; for reasons of self-interest they will labor for him and do his bidding. But in making us independent of others, money in the long run makes us dependent upon itself; it frees us from others in order to enslave us. LE.

Money, not being itself directly consumable and only a means of exchange for anything whatever, is an inducement to hoarding; for if I have a sum of money, I can make all kinds of plans for procuring for myself all sorts of objects and amenities in terms of which alone money is serviceable. LE.

MONOTHEISM Among all nations, even when still in a state of blind polytheism, we always see some sparks of monotheism, to which they have been led, not by meditation and profound speculation, but by the natural bent of the common reason, which they gradually followed and comprehended. CPuR.

MORAL Physical *well* or amoral *ill* implies only a reference to our condition, as pleasant or unpleasant; but *good* or *evil* always implies a reference to the moral law of spiritual reason. CPrR.

MORAL AND PHYSICAL If a man who delights in annoying and vexing peacable people, at last receives a heavy beating; this is no doubt a physically ill thing, but every one approves it and regards it as a morally good thing.   CPrR.

MORAL ARGUMENT The moral argument is not newly invented, only newly set forth. It has always lain undeveloped in the human mind.   CJ.

The moral argument does not claim to supply knowledge but merely faith.   CJ.

MORAL BEING That a person should deliberately lie to himself seems absurd and is difficult to understand. Man, a *moral* being, should not use himself, the physical being, merely as a talking machine, not concerned with the purpose of language. But he does so when, for example, he pretends to believe in a future world-judge, thinking that such confession can do no harm but might serve him well.
MM. *Vide* Afterlife.

MORAL CONCEPT Moral concepts may well serve as examples of pure concepts of reason.   CPuR.

MORAL CULTURE You consider moral culture as indispensable for physical health: such a view reveals the philosopher.
QuF.

The moral culture of man must begin, not with improvement in morals, but with a transformation of the mind and the foundation of a character.   RR.

MORAL EDUCATION An earnest representation of duty is more suited to progress in goodness. To set before children, as a pattern, actions that are called noble, magnanimous, meritorious, with the notion of captivating them by infusing an enthusiasm for such actions, is to defeat our end. For as they are still so backward in the observance of the commonest duty and even in the estimation of it, this means simply to make them fantastical romancers betimes. CPrR.

MORAL EMPLOYMENT The principles of reason possess objective reality in their practical and more particularly in their moral employment. CPuR.

MORAL EXISTENCE It is only man's moral existence which gives the existence of the world a purpose. CJ.

MORAL FOUNDATION The concept of good and evil must not be determined before the moral law, but only after it and by means of it. CPrR.

MORAL GROUND An intelligible cause only means the transcendental or moral ground. CPuR.

MORAL INTEREST The moral interest is a pure interest of practical reason alone, independent of sense. CPrR.

We see that the last intention of nature in her wise provision was really, in the constitution of our reason, directed to moral interests only. CPuR.

MORALITY Morality leads inevitably to religion. RR.

So sharply and clearly marked are the boundaries of morality and self-love, that even the commonest eye cannot fail to distinguish whether a thing belongs to the one or the other. CPrR.

Morality is in no need of religion. Morality is self-sufficient. RR.

The interest which the human mind takes in morality is

natural, though it is not undivided, and always practically preponderant. If you strengthen and increase that interest, you will find reason very docile, and even more enlightened, so as to be able to join the practical with the theoretical interests. If you do not take care that you first make men at least moderately good, you will never make them honest believers.   CPuR.

Morality, by itself, constitutes a system.   CPuR.
            Vide Moral Law; Moral World; Legality.

Morality is not properly the doctrine how we should make ourselves happy, but how we should become worthy of happiness.   CPrR.

Morality serves as a law for us only because we are rational beings.   FM. *Vide* Legality.

When human reason is tired, it likes to rest on amoral motives. In a dream of sweet illusions it embraces a cloud, mistaking it for Juno, and foists upon morality a bastard which resembles anything you please except morality.   FM.

Morality makes moral man out of physical man.   QuF.
                                    Vide Homo.

MORAL LAW Let us cherish none but good dispositions; let us exert ourselves to the utmost of our powers to comply with the moral law.   LE.

The moral law gives to the world of sense, which is a sensible system of nature, the form of a *world of reason*, that is, of a supersensible system.   CPrR.

Moral laws are expressed in the form 'thou shalt.'   LE.

A moral law states categorically what ought to be done, whether it pleases us or not. It is, therefore, not a case of

145

satisfying an inclination. If it were, there would be no moral law, but everyone might act according to his own feeling. LE.

Pure reason gives to man a universal law which we call the Moral Law. The fact just mentioned is undeniable. CPrR.

Pure practical laws, the object of which is given by reason entirely, and which convey commands, would be products of reason. Such are the moral laws, and these alone, therefore, belong to the sphere of the practical use of reason. CPuR.

The moral law remains binding upon every one. CPuR.

I assume that there really exist moral laws . . . . I feel justified in assuming this, by appealing, not only to the arguments of the most enlightened moralists, but also to the moral judgment of every man, if he only tries to conceive such a law clearly. CPuR.

Moral laws could not be commands if they did not connect adequate consequences with their rules, and carried with them both promises and threats. CPuR.

We shall show that the moral laws presuppose the existence of a Supreme Being. CPuR.

Unless we depend on moral laws, or are guided by them, there cannot be any theology of reason. CPuR.

The moral law is only possible under freedom. CJ.
Vide Dualism of Laws.

The laws of freedom, in contradistinction to the laws of nature, are called moral laws. MM.

MORAL MAXIM It is necessary that the whole course of our life should be subject to moral maxims. CPuR.

MORAL PERSONALITY Moral personality is freedom from the mechanism of nature, yet, regarded also as a faculty of a being which is subject to special laws. CPrR.
Vide Dualistic Philosophy.

MORAL PRINCIPLES Moral principles are necessary according to reason. CPuR.

MORAL QUALITY Man is either morally good or morally bad. RR.

MORALS Everybody has, if obscurely, a system of morals within himself and feels as if he could lay down the law. MM.

MORAL SATISFACTION In order that a rational being should will what reason alone directs such beings that they ought to will it is no doubt requisite that reason should have a power to infuse a feeling of pleasure or satisfaction in the fulfilment of duty. FM.

MORAL STRENGTH A mind inclined to widen its moral character feels a need for the existence of a divine being under whom our moral actions gain in strength and breadth. CJ.
Vide Morality.

MORAL UNITY When we refer external things to our own needs only we feel restricted as if a foreign *will* were operating in us, and a secret power compelled us to consider the welfare of others. We feel ourselves depending on the General Will, and from this springs moral unity following merely spiritual laws. DS.

MORAL VALUE The value of a person rests on the moral value of actions. CPrR.

147

Moral value does not depend on the sensuous actions which can be seen but on those innermost principles which cannot be seen. FM.

MORAL WISDOM Moral wisdom assumes easily but wrongly the prestige of being scientific. IK.

MORAL WORLD I call the world, in so far as it may be in accordance with moral laws which, by virtue of the rational beings it may, and according to the necessary laws of morality it ought to be, a moral world. This world is conceived as an intelligible world only. It is an idea which can and ought really to exercise its influence on the sensible world in order to bring it, as far as possible, into conformity with that idea. The idea of a moral world has objective reality. CPuR.

MORAL WORTH Moral worth or unworth of actions is possible by means of the value idea only. CPuR.

MORBIDITY The spirit of philosophy suggests the supreme dietetic task of mastering morbid feelings by mere determination. QuF.

MOROSENESS The ethics of moroseness assumes that all amenities of life and all pleasures of the senses are opposed to morality. LE.

MOTHER WIT The faculty of judgment is a special talent which cannot be taught, but must be practiced. This is what constitutes our so-called mother wit, the absence of which cannot be remedied by any schooling. For although the teacher may offer, and as it were graft into a narrow understanding, plenty of rules borrowed from the experience of others, the faculty of using them rightly must belong to the pupil himself, and without that talent no present that may be given is safe from abuse. CPuR.

MOTION Motion is a pure act of successive synthesis of the manifold in external intuition in general by means of productive imagination. CPuR.

MOTIVE Motives are springs of the will which are drawn from the senses. LE.

MUNDANE OBJECT All mundane objects are nothing but phenomena. CPuR.

MURDER When a man has killed another it does not necessarily follow that he has murdered him. LE.

MURDERER If a man has committed murder, he must die; there is no other substitute to satisfy justice. MM.

MUTILATION To deprive oneself of an integral part or organ, e. g., to give away or sell a tooth to be transplanted into another person's mouth, or to submit oneself to castration in order to gain a more comfortable livelihood as a singer, and so on, belongs to partial self-murder. MM.
Vide Hair.

MYSTERY A certain degree of mystery even in a book is welcome to any reader because it makes him enjoy his own perspicacity when he penetrates the fog. A.

MYSTIQUE OF NUMBERS A strange play of the imagination lies in the mystique of numbers, often combination between the numbers seven and nine. It looks as if the Jewish-Christian chronology had not adjusted itself to history but history adapted itself to the chronology. A.

N

NATIVES When they discovered America, the Negro lands, the Spice Islands, the Cape etc., they regarded these lands as belonging to nobody, for them the natives counted as nobody.   PP.

NATURAL NECESSITY The necessity of natural phenomena may be called natural necessity.   CPuR.

NATURAL PHENOMENA Extension and impermeability furnish the highest empirical principle of the unity of natural phenomena.   CPuR.

NATURAL STATE The state of peace among men is not the natural state; the natural state is one of war.   PP.

NATURE Many powers of nature, which manifest their existence by certain effects remain perfectly inscrutable to us, because we cannot follow them up far enough by observation.   CPuR.

It must be the same to you, when you do perceive it, whether we say, God has wisely willed it so, or *nature* has wisely arranged it so.   CPuR.

There exists a sublime and wise ground which must be the condition of the *world*, not only as a blind and all-powerful nature, by means of unconscious fecundity, but as an intelligence, by freedom. CPuR.

Whatever has been ordained by nature is good for some purpose or other. Even poisons serve to counteract other poisons which are in our blood, and they must not be absent therefore in a complete collection of medicines. CPuR.

Nature is the sum total of all phenomena . . . a lawful order of phenomena. CPuR.

Nature displays her procedure in her tiniest as in her largest parts. GTH.

While exalting nature, people try at the same time to belittle her. GTH.

If God allowed nature in certain cases to deviate from its laws, our reason would be paralyzed and could not hope to be ever instructed about the matter. RR.

NATURE AND FREEDOM Nature and freedom can without contradiction be attributed to the very same thing, but in different relations, on one side as a natural phenomenon, on the other as a thing in itself. PM.

NAUGHTINESS Naughtiness is in a way a sign of strength and only requires discipline; but any secret deceitful viciousness contains no seed of good. LE.

NECESSARIES Man must discipline his mind in regard to the necessaries of life. LE.

NECESSARY That of which the existence is unconditioned is called necessary. CPuR.

152

NECESSITY If we admit the existence of something, we must also admit that something exists by necessity. CPuR.

All our actions may be necessitated in two ways. They may be necessary in accordance with normative laws, when their necessity is practical; or of our sensuous inclination, when their necessity is psychological. LE.

Now the unconditioned necessity of moral judgments is not the same thing as the conditioned necessity of natural things. CPuR.

Necessity cannot cancel morality. LE.

NECESSITY, MORAL The intelligible or moral idea, the necessity of which neither requires nor admits of any empirical condition, is, as regards natural phenomena, unconditionally necessary. CPuR. *Vide* Freedom.

NECESSITY, NATURAL As there certainly is something that follows, I must necessarily refer it to something else which precedes, and upon which it follows by rule, that is, by necessity. CPuR.

NECESSITY AND FREEDOM If natural necessity is referred merely to physical phenomena, and freedom merely to things in themselves, no contradiction arises. PM.

I may say: all natural phenomena are subject to the necessity of nature; but . . . rational reason is free. PM.

NEEDS Many are our needs, or things we have made our needs. LE.

NEGATION No one can definitely think a negation, unless he founds it on the opposite affirmation. A man born blind cannot frame the smallest conception of darkness, because he has none of light. The savage knows nothing of poverty, because he does not know ease, and the ignorant has no conception of his ignorance, because he has none of knowledge etc. All negative concepts are therefore derivative.

CPuR.

NEGATIVE PROPOSITION Negative propositions, intended to prevent erroneous knowledge in cases where error is never possible, may no doubt be very true, but they are empty, they do not answer any purpose, and sound therefore often absurd; like the well-known utterance of a rhetorician, that Alexander could not have conquered any countries without an army.

CPuR.

NEIGHBOR It is a good thing to love one's neighbor: it makes us good-natured; but how can we love him if he is not lovable? In such a case, love cannot be an inclination, but must be a wish in which we could find pleasure. If we seek for it, we shall surely discover something lovable in them, just as an unlovable man finds in others, because he looks for them, the qualities which make them unlovable.

LE.

It can be said with full justification that we ought to love our neighbor.

LE.

NEUTRALITY A skeptical use of pure reason might be called the principle of neutrality in all its disputes.

CPuR.

NEW It is hardly to be expected that we should not be able to match every new thing with some old thing not unlike it.

PM.

We have been long accustomed to seeing antiquated knowledge produced as new, by being taken out of its former

154

context, and fitted into a suit of any fancy pattern, under new titles. PM.

NEWS If a man spreads false news, though he does no wrong to anyone in particular, he offends against mankind, because if such a practice were universal man's desire for knowledge would be frustrated. LE.

NIGGARDLINESS To be niggardly with things which can be directly enjoyed and used, like food and old clothes, is therefore the meanest kind of avarice. LE.

NOTHING COMES FROM NOTHING The proposition, from nothing comes nothing, was only another conclusion from the same principle of permanence, or rather of the constant presence of the real subject in phenomena. CPuR.

NOUMENON What is the reason why people, not satisfied with the substratum of sensibility, have added to the natural phenomena the noumena or spiritual values, which the understanding only is supposed to be able to realize? It really follows quite naturally from the concept of a phenomenon, that something must correspond to it, which in itself is not a phenomenon, but a noumenon. CPuR.

If I admit things or spiritual values which are objects of the understanding only, and not of sensuous intuition, such things would be called Noumena. CPuR.
Vide Phenomenon and Noumenon.

The concept of a noumenon or a spiritual value, that is of a thing which can never be thought as an object of the senses, but only as a thing by itself, is not self-contradictory. CPuR.

NOVELIST A novelist lets his heroine flee to remote countries, there to meet, by a lucky chance, her admirer.   DS.

NUMBER The pure schema of quantity is number. Number is nothing but the unity of the synthesis of the manifold of a homogeneous intuition in general.   CPuR.

O

OATH That people should be legally compelled to profess that there are gods can have no other reason than to make them take an oath.   **MM.**

OBEDIENCE I must obey the moral law on all points.   **CPuR.**

OBJECT We may indeed call everything, even every representation, so far as we are conscious of it, an object.   **CPuR.**

OBJECTION All objections may be divided into dogmatical, critical, and sceptical. The dogmatical attacks the proposition, the critical the proof of a proposition.   **CPuR.**
Vide Sceptical Objection.

OBJECTIVITY Our conception of the relation of all *knowledge* to its object contains something of necessity, the object being looked upon as that which prevents our knowledge from being determined at haphazard.   **CPuR.**

OBLIGATION So far as practical reason is entitled to lead us we shall not look upon actions as obligatory because they are the commands of God, but look upon them as divine commands because we feel an inner obligation to follow them.   **CPuR.**

OBSCURITY Studied obscurity is sometimes successfully used for simulating profundity—as objects seen in twilight or through a mist always appear larger than they are.   **A.**

OBSERVATION New observations add and remove certain predicates, so that the concept never stands within safe limits.
CPuR.

A man who feels himself watched either is too embarrassed to show his true nature or tries to conceal it. A.

OCCUPATION Life is the faculty of spontaneous activity, the awareness of all our human powers. Occupation gives us this awareness. LE.

OFFENSE What anyone does that is less than the law demands is moral offense. MM.

OLD Old people are full of complaints. EO.

Getting old does not require external and violent causes; the same causes which bring a thing to perfection drive it in imperceptible stages on to its extinction. EO.

Old age tries by means of the artificial power of money to make up for its lack of physical strength and power. LE.

To become old is a great sin, and we are ruthlessly punished for it by death. Old age entails frequent procrastination of important resolutions. One such is the resolution to die. Death always announces himself too soon for us, and we never tire of finding excuses for letting him wait. QuF.

OMISSION Moral omissions and their consequences can never be imputed, but legal omissions can. LE.

ONANISM Onanism is abuse; the exercise of the faculty in the complete absence of any object of sexuality. The practice is contrary to the ends of humanity and even opposed to animal nature. LE.

158

ONTOLOGY The proud name of Ontology, which presumes to supply in a systematic form different kinds of synthetical knowledge a priori, must be replaced by the more modest name of a mere Analytic of the pure understanding. CPuR.

OPINION In the judgments of pure understanding *opinion* is not permitted . . . . Hence it is absurd to have an opinion in pure mathematics; here one must either know, or abstain from pronouncing any judgment. CPuR.

OPIUM Opium renders man dumb and incommunicative and is only permitted as medicine. MM.

OPPOSITES Opposites cannot exist at the same time in the same thing, but only one after the other. CPuR.

OPPOSITION The real in the phenomena may very well be in mutual opposition, and if connected in one subject, one may annihilate completely or in part the effect of the other, as in the case of two forces moving in the same straight line, either drawing or impelling a point in opposite directions, or in the case of pleasure, counterbalancing a certain amount of pain. CPuR.

ORDER Natural theology ascends to the highest intelligence as the principle either of all natural or of all moral order. CPuR.

ORDER, NATURAL Order and design in nature must themselves be explained on natural grounds and according to natural laws; and for this purpose even the wildest hypotheses, if only they are physical, are more tolerable than a hyperphysical one,—that is, the appeal to the Divine Author. CPuR.

ORGANIC The origin of the entire present inorganic world-structure will be understood, before the organic production of one single blade of grass by mechanical causes will be distinctly known. GTH.

ORGANIC BODY In an organic body, every member exists for the sake of all others, and all others exist for the sake of the one. CPuR.

ORGANISM Everything in a organism is good for something. CJ.

ORGANIZATION It is only an issue of a good organization that the powers of each selfish disposition are so arranged in opposition that one moderates or even destroys the disastrous effect of the other. PP.

ORGANUM An Organum of pure understanding ought to comprehend all the principles by which pure knowledge can be acquired and fully established. A complete application of such an Organum would give us a System of Pure Understanding. CPuR.

ORIGIN Origin is the derivation of a consequence from its primary condition, that is, one which is not in its turn a consequence of another condition. . . . It is a contradiction then to seek for the time-origin of free actions; or of the moral character of man, because the principle of freedom must be sought for in conceptions of reason. RR.

ORTHODOXY The orthodox assert that their own conception of religion must necessarily be right and ought to be universal; but what is orthodoxy? If we were all to appear before the gates of heaven and the question were put to us, 'Which of you is orthodox?' the Jew, the Turk, and the Christian would shout in unison, 'I am.' Orthodoxy should use force against no one. LE.

160

OUGHT The 'ought' always designates the quality of goodness and not of pleasantness.   LE.

We must do what is in our power; we must do what we ought; the rest we should leave to God.   LE.

Whatsoever we do is done not for God's benefit, but for our own: we do what we ought.   LE.

The ought expresses a kind of necessity and connection with grounds, which we do not find elsewhere in the whole of nature or of natural causes. The understanding can know in nature only what is present, past, or future. It is impossible that anything in it ought to be different from what it is in reality. Nay, if we only look at the course of nature, the ought has no meaning whatever. We cannot ask, what ought to be in nature, as little as we can ask, what qualities a circle ought to possess. We can only ask what happens in it, and what qualities that which happens has.   CPuR.

The ought expresses a possible action, the condition of which cannot be anything but a mere conceptual or spiritual ground, while in every merely natural action the condition must always be a causal or physical phenomenon. There may be ever so many natural causes which impel me to will and ever so many sensuous temptations, but they can never produce the supersensuous ought, but only a willing which is always conditioned, and against which the unconditioned or causefree ought, pronounced by reason, sets measure, ay, prohibition and authority. Intelligible reason does not yield to the impulse that is given empirically, and does not follow the order of things, as they present themselves as natural phenomena, but frames for itself, with perfect spontaneity, a new order according to spiritual ideas or transcendental grounds to which it adapts the empirical conditions, and according to which it declares

161

actions to be morally necessary, even though they have not taken place. CPuR. *Vide* Freedom and Causality.

OUGHT AND IS The former arrives at a conclusion that something is because something ought to take place; the latter, that something is because something does take place. CPuR.

OUTWARD RELIGION The term outward religion is contradictory. Religion must be inward; actions may be outward, but they do not constitute religion and they in no wise serve God; actions directed to God are nothing but means for strengthening the disposition of surrender to God. LE.

OUTWITTING With regard to the senses generally, as they outwit and cheat the understanding, we can do nothing else than outwit them in turn by doing our best to offer to the mind an alternative entertainment to that offered by the senses. We must try to occupy the mind with ideal pleasures. LE.

OVERCHARGING Wherever there is much commerce the prudent tradesman does not overcharge, but keeps a fixed price for every one so that a child buys of him as well as any other person. FM.

P

PAINTED STATUES We detest *painted statues*; they betray us into thinking they are alive.   **A.**

PAINTING He who paints nature either with brush or pen is not a bel esprit, for he only imitates; he who paints ideas is alone a master of beauty in art.   **A.**

PARADOX Paradox has its uses; it should not be used to clinch a special point, but only to put a new face upon a particular view; it is the unexpected in thought which often puts the mind upon a new track.   **LE.** *Vide* Wit.

Paradoxes, even if born from perversity, shake up the mind and may lead to discovery; whereas that which is commonplace and has public opinion on its side, lulls you to sleep.   **A.**

PARASITE Do not be a parasite nor a flatterer nor a beggar.   **MM.**

PARENTS Between parents and children there must be a respect which should continue throughout life, and this rules out of court any question of equality.   **LE.**

PARLIAMENT The people are supposed to be represented by their deputies in parliament, who ought to be trustees of their liberties and rights. But these persons are too intensely interested in providing offices for themselves and their families.   **MM.**

163

PARSIMONY Parsimony in principle is not only considered as an economical rule of reason, but as an essential law of nature.   CPuR.

PASSION No man is sane when swayed by passion; his inclination is blind and cannot be in keeping with the dignity of mankind. We must, therefore, altogether avoid giving way to passion.   LE.

PATIENCE We must learn to bear the discomforts of life and to test our strength in suffering them with patience and without losing our contentment; if we bear with a cheerful mind and a happy disposition the ills which cannot be altered, we have strength of mind.   LE.

We may be submissive and patient because we must, because we cannot alter things and complaint is in vain.   LE.

PEACE A state of peace must be *established*, for in order to be secured against enmity it is not sufficient that hostilities simply cease.   PP.

In a state of peace laws have force.   PP.

PEACE-LOVING There are two ways in which a man can be peace-loving: he may wish for his own peace and he may strive to bring peace to others. The latter is the more noble of the two.   LE.

PEACE OF MIND When the reflective man has triumphed over temptations to vice and is conscious of having done his often difficult duty, he finds himself in a state of contentment and peace of mind which can well be called happiness and in which virtue is its own reward.   MM.

PEDANT When pedants presume to address the public in the technical terms that are suitable only for the schools, the

164

philosopher cannot be blamed any more than the grammarian for the folly of the quibbler. The ridicule here can hit only a man, not the science.   MM.

PENANCE There is no virtue in practices of the kind, such as doing penance and fasting, which merely waste the body; they are fanatical and monkish virtues.   LE.

PEOPLE The people ask: if I have lived a wicked life, how can I quickly, before the gate is closed, get a ticket of admission to the heavenly kingdom? If I am in the wrong, how can I nevertheless win my lawsuit? If I have misused my bodily forces to my heart's delight, how can I still remain in good health and live long? You scholars, you must know!   QuF.

The mental characters of peoples are most discernible by whatever in them is moral.   BS.

PERCEPTION Perception is empirical consciousness, that is, a consciousness in which there is at the same time sensation.   CPuR.

PERFECT It requires the concept of that which is perfect of its kind, in order to estimate and measure by it the degree and the number of the defects in the imperfect.   CPuR.

PERFECTION Human perfection consists not only in the cultivation of the mind but also in that of the will.   MM.

The idea of perfection is a proper standard, and if we measure our worth by it, we find that we fall short of it and feel that we must exert ourselves to come nearer to it.   LE.

Complete unity of design constitutes perfection. If we do not find such perfection in the general and necessary laws

165

of nature, how shall we thence infer the idea of a supreme and absolutely necessary perfection of an original Being, as the origin of all causality? CPuR.

PERMANENCE As all effect consists in that which happens, that is, in the changeable, indicating time in succession, the last subject of it is the permanent, as the substratum of all that changes, that is substance. CPuR.

PERMANENCE, PRINCIPLE OF In all changes of phenomena the substance is permanent, and its quantum is neither increased nor diminished in nature. CPuR.

PERPETUAL PEACE The guarantee of perpetual peace is nothing less than nature. PP.

PERSECUTION The spirit of persecution, when it is secret and works behind a man's back, discussing him and calling him an atheist, is a spirit of meanness. But it may be refined, so that it does not persecute with hatred those who are not of its opinion, but merely abhors them. LE.

PERSON The physical person who belongs to the world of the senses is also subject to his own moral personality because he belongs at the same time to the spiritual or *moral* world. CPrR.

The value of a person rests on the moral value of his actions. CPrR.

I am conscious of myself. . . . This thought contains a two fold 'I', one as subject and one as object. . . . Only the I who thinks is the person. The I as an object, is simply a thing like all others which are outside me.
Advances in Philosophy since Leibniz and Wolff.

A person or an action can be good or evil, but a thing can never be so called. CPrR.

We are, as human beings, not things but persons, and by turning ourselves into things we dishonor human nature in our own persons. LE.

A person is a subject whose actions are capable of being imputed. MM. *Vide* Thing.

PERSONALITY Identity, as that of an intellectual substance, gives us personality. CPuR.

PERSUASION If a judgment has its ground in the peculiar character of the subject only, it is called persuasion. CPuR.

PETTIFOGGER Our pettifogger engages in all manner of legal quibbles; he makes use of the letter of the law for his own purposes; when dealing with facts he pays no heed to disposition, but only to external circumstances; he deals in probabilities. LE.

PHENOMENA Natural phenomena are not things by themselves. CPuR. *Vide* the Introduction; Appearance.

The undefined object of an empirical intuition is called phenomenon. CPuR.

There is no reason why we should not simply derive the phenomena of the natural world and their existence from other phenomena, as if there were no necessary spiritual Being at all, while at the same time we might always strive towards the completeness of that derivation, just as if such a Being, as the highest ground, were presupposed. CPuR.

Wherever there is action, activity and force, there must

be substance, and in this alone the seat of that fertile source of phenomena can be sought. CPuR.

A house is not a thing by itself but a natural phenomenon. CPuR. *Vide* the Introduction.

PHENOMENON AND NOUMENON One might feel inclined to feel that the concept of natural Phenomena suggested by itself the objective reality of the spiritual values or Noumena, and justified a division of objects into phenomena and noumena, and consequently of the world into a sensible and intelligible world. CPuR.

PHENOMENA, INNER People mistake inner phenomena for external experiences, perhaps inspired by a nonsensuous agent. Often people indulge deliberately in insane daydreams, thinking them a wholesome antidote against low sensuality. A.

PHILANTHROPIST He who takes pleasure when things go well with other people is called a friend of men in general. MM.

PHILAUTIA If a man believes himself kindhearted and promotes the welfare of all mankind by empty wishes, he is a prey to philautia. LE.

PHILOSOPHER Although the proper counselor for patients is the physician, I should not like to exclude the philosopher, who could prescribe a dietetic for the mind, but of course he must not demand a fee. DH.

Kings and king-like peoples should not suffer the philosophers be silent, but should let them speak openly. PP.

Since the philosophers are by nature incapable of lobbying and plotting, they are above suspicion of being made up of propagandists. PP.

168

A philosopher generally expresses himself somewhat more definitely.   CPuR.

To eat his meals alone with his own thoughts does not bring relaxation to a philosopher; he should be gaily entertained by a table companion with new and varying matters and ideas.   A.

Those who enquire into concepts will admit. . . .   CPuR.

PHILOSOPHICAL Knowledge of reason, derived from concepts, is called philosophical.   CPuR.

PHILOSOPHICAL DUALISM   *Vide* Dualistic Philosophy.

PHILOSOPHICAL KNOWLEDGE Philosophical knowledge considers the particular in the general only, mathematical, the general in the particular.   CPuR.

PHILOSOPHIZING Philosophizing, even when one is not a philosopher, provides the mind with an interesting occupation and prevents stagnation. Genuine philosophy produces a feeling of strength which may compensate for bodily frailties by a rational estimate of the value of life.   QuF.

PHILOSOPHY Provided only she is not chased away or gagged, philosophy wants nothing but to be free and to leave others free to find out the truth for the benefit of all.   QuF.

The legislation of human understanding has two objects only: the law of nature and the law of morals. The philosophy of nature relates to all that is; that of morals to that only that ought to be.   CPuR.

Inasmuch as there can be only one human understanding, so likewise there cannot be many philosophies; only one true system of philosophy is possible, however variously and even contradictorily men may have philosophized over one and the same proposition.   MM.

Philosophy swarms with faulty definitions, particularly such as contain some true elements of a definition, but not all.
CPuR.

All philosophy is either knowledge derived from pure reason, or knowledge derived from empirical principles.
CPuR.

Philosophy is either theoretical or practical. It is the object that differentiates them.
LE.

PHILOSOPHY AND COMMON UNDERSTANDING I ask, do you really require that knowledge, which concern all men, should go beyond the common understanding, and should be revealed to you by philosophers only? In matters which concern all men without distinction, nature cannot be accused of any partial distribution of her gifts; the highest philosophy can achieve no more than that guidance which nature has vouchsafed even to the meanest understanding.
CPuR.

PHILOSOPHY AND GEOMETRY The art of measuring, or geometry, will by its method produce nothing in philosophy but card-houses, while the philosopher with his method produces in mathematics nothing but vain babble.   CPuR.

PHRASEOLOGY Habitual phraseological padding, used to fill the emptiness of thoughts, keeps the listener constantly waiting for that pet phrase and the speaker seems like a talking-machine.   A.

PHYSICAL AND MORAL The man who submits to a surgical operation, feels it no doubt as a physically ill thing, but by their reason he and every one acknowledge it to be morally good.   CPrR.

PHYSICIAN I shall imitate the method of the physicians who

170

think they have been most useful to their patients if they give their disease a name. **DH.**

PHYSICS The metaphysics of corporeal nature is called physics. **CPuR.**

It took a much longer time before physics entered on the highway of science. **CPuR.**

PHYSIOLOGY Immanent physiology considers nature as the sum total of all objects of the senses. **CPuR.**

PIETY Piety, which is practical, consists in obeying the divine laws for the reason that God wills it. **LE.**

PLAN Making plans is oft the occupation of a luxurious and boastful mind, which thus obtains the reputation of a creative genius, by demanding what it cannot itself supply; by censuring, what it cannot improve; and by proposing, what it knows not where to find. **PM.**

We have been warned not to venture blindly on a plan which may be beyond our powers. **CPuR.**

PLANETARY INHABITANTS To assume rational inhabitants on other planets is a matter of opinion; some time it may be possible for us to come nearer to them. **CJ.**

PLATO Plato discovered his ideas principally in what is practical. **CPuR.**

PLATONIC REPUBLIC The Platonic Republic has been supposed to be a striking example of purely imaginary perfection. It has become a byword, as something that could exist in the brain of an idle thinker only, and Brucker thinks it ridiculous that Plato could have said that no prince could ever govern well, unless he participated in the value ideas. We should do better, however, to follow up this

171

thought and endeavor to place it in a clearer light by our own efforts, rather than to throw it aside as useless, under the miserable and very dangerous pretext of its impracticability.   CPuR.

PLAY It is better to be occupied in play than not to be occupied at all; for by play we at least sustain our energies.   LE.

He who has lost at play may be vexed at himself and his folly, but if he is conscious of having cheated at play, he must despise himself as soon as he compares himself with the moral law.   CPrR.

Play is wisely introduced by nature to spur individuals to competitive and daring feats. Two contestants may think that they play together, but in reality nature plays with them.   A.

PLEASANT What is pleasant is a matter of individual appreciation.   LE.

PLEASANTNESS When we inquire what are the determining grounds of desire, and place them in some expected pleasantness, it is of no consequence whence the idea of this pleasing object is derived, but only how much it pleases.
                                                                CPrR.

PLEASURE The pleasures of life do not fill time full, but leave it empty.   LE.

The agreeable, the beautiful, and the good signify three different relations to the feeling of pleasure. The agreeable is relished, the beautiful pleases, and the good is appreciated as objectively valuable.   CJ.

POEM To end a poem with a verse that can be stored in memory as a motto causes pleasure in the aftertaste and thus belongs to the art of the poet.   A.

POET Poets make no such fortune as lawyers and men of other learned professions.   A.

POINT The centre of a circle, or any mathematical point, is defined, but it cannot actually be made small enough to comply with the definition.   LE.

POLEMICS By the polemical use of pure understanding I mean the defense of its own propositions against dogmatical negations.   CPuR.

POLITENESS Can an untruth from mere politeness be considered as lying?   MM.

POLITICIAN The practical politician takes the attitude of looking down with great self-satisfaction on the political theorist as a pedant whose empty ideas in no way endanger the security of the state; so the theorist is allowed to play his game without interference from the worldly-wise statesman.   PP.

A political artist can rule the world by the power of imagination.   A.

POLITICS Politics says, "Be ye wise as serpents"; morality adds, as a qualified condition, "and guileless as doves."   PP.

All politics must bend its knee before the right. But thus it can hope to arrive at the stage where it shines with an immortal glory.   PP.

POOR If a man has only sufficient for his barest necessities he is poor, and if he has not sufficient even for these he is needy.   LE.

POPULARIZATION This wise man [Garve] rightly expects that a philosophical book be capable of being popularized. MM.

POSSESSION No man would willingly give away all his possessions; but he will do so if this be the only way whereby he can save his children.   LE.

In the possession of virtue a man is free, healthy, rich, because he possesses himself and that is a possession he cannot lose.   A.

POSSESSION AND PROPERTY Children can never be the property of the parents, yet they are their possession.   MM.

POSSIBILITY What agrees with the formal conditions of experience is possible.   CPuR.

This is a warning against inferring at once from the possibility of concepts the possibility of things.   CPuR.

POSTPONEMENT Postponement of your lust will make you richer; the profit will be yours. The consciousness that you have the enjoyment in your control is more fruitful than anything that satisfies the senses by consuming them.   A.
                                                      Vide Sexual Love.

POSTULATE, MATHEMATICAL To postulate should mean to represent a proposition as certain without proof or justification.   CPuR.

POWER The possession of power unavoidably corrupts the unrestrained judgment of reason.   PP.

The origin of supreme power is unfathomable.   MM.

Great powers blush only at the judgment of other great powers but not at that of the common people.   PP.

The causality of a substance we call power. CPuR.

PRACTICAL I call practical whatever is possible through freedom. CPuR.

PRACTICAL FREEDOM Practical freedom presupposes that,
although something has not happened, it *ought* to have
happened. CPuR. *Vide* Ought.

Freedom, in its practical sense, is the independence of the
will from the coercion through sensuous impulses. CPuR.

PRACTICAL IDEA The practical or moral idea is truly fruitful,
and, with regard to practical conduct, indispensable and
necessary. In it reason becomes a ground and active power,
capable of realizing what is contained in its concept. CPuR.

PRACTICAL LAW There are practical laws. CPuR.

PRACTICAL REASON Practical reason is itself the moral lawgiver. CJ.

PRACTICAL RULE The practical rule is always a product of
reason, because it prescribes action as a means to the
effect. CPrR.

PRAGMATIC Practical philosophy is pragmatic in respect of the
laws of prudence. LE.

PRAYER There is a widespread opinion that, as God knows our
wants better than we do ourselves, there is no need to pray.
Objectively, prayer is certainly unnecessary. Whether or not
we express our creature-wishes in words, God knows them.
Subjectively, however, prayer is necessary. It is necessary
for our own sake. LE.

Frequently ordinary people can only pray aloud. They are

incapable of silent thought, and loud prayer impresses them; but persons accustomed to unfold their minds in silence stand in no need of praying aloud. LE.

The spirit of prayer subsists without the letter. LE.

Prayer trains us to act aright: it is merely an exercise for good action, but is not in itself such an action. LE.

PREACHER There should be an examination for preachers, not only to test their knowledge of dogmatics, but equally to test their character and heart. LE.

PRECEPT Precepts, not the example of others, should be the ground of our actions. LE.

PRECISION Scholastic precision must be insisted upon, even if such precision is denounced as hairsplitting. MM.

PREDICATES Phenomenal predicates can be attributed to the object in its relation to our sense: as for instance to the rose its red color, and its scent. CPuR.

I cannot bestow on a nonsensuous being predicates which are valid only in the world of the senses. CJ.

By whatever and by however many predicates I may think a thing, nothing is really added to it, if I add that the thing exists. Otherwise, it would not be the same that exists, but something more than was contained in the concept, and I could not say that the exact object of my concept existed. CPuR. *Vide* Reality and Possibility.

PREDISPOSITION, HUMAN Many have asserted that the predisposition in man is not to good but to evil. LE.

PREJUDICE The eternal prejudices of the schools are more

obstinate, absurd, and silly than the common prejudices.
IM.

PRETENSE Only in ourselves must all pretense of goodness be wiped out and the veil covering our own moral defects torn completely away. A.

PRIDE The proud man does not underrate his fellows, but he insists upon his own merits; he will not bow and scrape before them; he considers that he has a definite worth and will yield to none in that respect. Such pride is right and proper, provided it is kept within bounds. LE.

This self-respect in comparison with others constitutes noble pride. A low opinion of oneself in relation to others is no humility; it is a sign of a little spirit and of a servile character. . . . This form of humility is in fact a form of pride. LE.

PRIMITIVE CULTURE The more primitive the social culture the more necessary are special associations. LE.

PRINCIPLE, A PRIORI Principles a priori are so called, not only because they contain the grounds for other judgments, but also because they themselves are not founded on higher and more general kinds of knowledge. CPuR.

PRINCIPLE OF SUFFICIENT REASON All possible experience, that is, all objective knowledge of phenomena with regard to their relation in the succession of time, depends on 'the principle of sufficient reason.' CPuR.

PRINTING The eyes of the reader should be protected against bad printing and bad paper. At present, by a wretched affection of the printers the eyes are assaulted from all sides. The printer's ink is grey instead of black to make it look more gentle. And they choose the smallest type possible so that the even more minute type of the footnotes is only just legible. QuF.

PROBABILITY Probability is a kind of truth, known through insufficient causes, the knowledge of which is therefore deficient, but not deceitful. CPuR.

PROGRESS, HUMAN We maintain, in defiance of all unbelievers, that the human race always did progress and will go on progressing, provided we watch what is going on in all nations of the earth. QuF.

PROLONGING LIFE This is where the art of prolonging life has led: that in the end one is just tolerated among the living. QuF.

PROOF Of every proof, empirical or rational, we must demand that it should not persuade or beguile the mind but convince it. CJ.

PROPER CHARACTERISTICS I often see even intelligent men quarrelling with each other about the characteristic distinctions of men, animals, or plants, nay, even of minerals, the one admitting the existence of certain tribal characteristics, while others insist that nature has made the same provision for all, and that all differences are due to accidental environment. But they need only consider the nature of the object, in order to understand that it is far too deeply hidden for both of them to enable them to speak from a real insight into the nature of the object. CPuR.

PROPHESY How is it possible to prophesy the course of history? Answer: if the prophet himself brings about the events he prophesies. QuF.

PROPRIETY Civilized propriety is the garment of morality. A.

PROSPERITY I see that another is prosperous and I am pleased, but it is not his good fortune which should please me as much as the actual steps and conduct which have brought it about. LE.

PROSTITUTION To let one's person out on hire and to surrender it to another for the satisfaction of his sexual desire in return for money is the depth of infamy. LE.

PROVIDENCE In the course of the world taken as a whole everything is grounded in His good providence, and we may hope that everything, in general, happens in accordance with the foresight of God. LE.

Why has Providence placed certain things, which concern our highest interests, so far beyond our reach that we are only able to apprehend them very indistinctly and dubiously, and our enquiring gaze is more excited than satisfied by them? CPuR.

PRUDENCE Prudence is the ability to use the means towards the universal end of men, that is, happiness. LE.

In the teaching of prudence, the whole business of reason consists in concentrating all the objects of our desires in one, namely, happiness. CPuR.

PRUSSIAN INFANTRY The Prussian infantry is trained to put the left foot first as if on a hypomochlion (fulcrum) in order to perform the swing of the attack with the right side.
On the Power of the Mind to Master Morbidity.

PSEUDO-FRIENDSHIP The friendship of taste is a pseudo-friendship. It consists in the pleasure we derive from each other's company, and not from each other's happiness. LE.

PSEUDO-NECESSITIES The more dependent we are on pseudo-necessities, the more is our contentment at their mercy. LE.

179

PSYCHOLOGY The study of the soul. CPuR.

The thinking subject is the object-matter of *psychology*. CPuR.

PUBLIC, THE If on the one side the public has no understanding for the fine-drawn arguments in support of useful truths, it is not troubled on the other by the equally subtle objections. CPuR.

The public does not participate in the subtle investigations of philosophy. CPrR.

PUDICITY Pudicity, concealing passion, is a wholesome pretense which keeps distance between the sexes and does not demean one partner into becoming the tool of the other's lust. A.

PUN Puns are a shallow kind of wit. A.

PUNISHMENT Punishments must be in keeping with the nobility of mind. They must not be insulting or contemptuous; otherwise they induce an ignoble type of character. LE.

Punishment in general is physical evil accruing from moral evil. It is either deterrent or else retributive. LE.

The holy law implies of necessity that punishment should fit the crime. But in view of man's moral infirmity, is there to be no help for him? Assuredly there is. He can place his hope in a benevolent ruler. LE.

It is quite rational to say, that in a perfect state no punishments would be necessary. CPuR.

PUPIL The pupil becomes acquainted with names only, the meaning and application of which he has to learn afterwards. CPuR.

180

PURE REASON No given action can begin absolutely by itself. Of pure reason, however, we cannot say that the state in which it determines the will is preceded by another, in which that state itself is determined. For as timeless reason itself is not a natural phenomenon, and not subject to any of the conditions of sensibility, there exists in it no succession of time, and the law of nature, which determines the succession of time according to rules, cannot be applied to it. CPuR.

PURITY If we mix it with other drinks we are unable to taste the pure wine. So it is with morality. If we are to appreciate it, we must keep it pure and free from admixtures which are only in the way. LE.

PURPOSE The purposes of the Godhead must be determined by God. How should we dictate the purpose of the world? LE.

By a purpose I mean an object to be brought into existence as a result of a normative concept. CJ.

The conception of a purpose of nature points to an order of things completely different from mere mechanism. CJ.

Things which are effects presuppose other things as causes. But the concept of purposes supposes cause-free spiritual values. CJ.

181

Q

QUANTITY, INTENSIVE Every reality in a phenomenon has intensive quantity, that is, a degree. CPuR.

QUESTION It is a great and necessary proof of wisdom and sagacity to know what questions may be reasonably asked. For if a question is absurd in itself and calls for an answer where there is no answer, it does not only throw disgrace on the questioner, but often tempts an uncautious listener into absurd answers, thus presenting, as the ancients said, the spectacle of one person milking a he-goat, and of another holding the sieve. CPuR.

R

RAILLERY Raillery lowers our self-esteem more than malice, for it makes us a laughingstock for others, strips us of our worth and holds us up to ridicule.   LE.

RAPE If a woman cannot preserve her life any longer except by surrendering her person to the will of another, she is bound to give up her life rather than dishonor humanity in her own person, which is what she would be doing in giving herself up as a thing to the will of another.   LE.

RATIO IGNAVA This would be a principle of ratio ignava [lazy understanding], to pass by all causes the objective reality of which may be known by continued experience, in order to rest on a mere idea.   CPuR.

RATIONAL BEING Everything in nature works according to laws. Rational beings alone have the faculty of acting according to the conception of laws, that is, according to *principles.*   FM.

RATIONAL NATURE *Rational nature exists* as an end in itself.   FM.

Rational nature is distinguished from the rest of nature by this, that it sets before itself an end.   FM.

READER The reader has a right to demand not only what may be called logical or discursive clearness, which is based on concepts, but also what may be called aesthetic or intuitive clearness produced by intuitions, i. e., by examples and concrete illustrations. CPuR.

READING PUBLIC The ravenous appetite of our reading public of refined taste is always kept eager by ephemeral writings which leave the heads entirely empty while giving the reader's busy idleness the appearance of work done. A.

REALITY *Reality* is that which corresponds to a sensation in general: that, therefore, the concept of which indicates by itself being. CPuR.

We might assume that in the world of natural phenomena everything appears to follow mechanical laws, while the teleological principles have their origin in the nonsensuous ground. Thus both principles might have objective *reality* side by side. CJ.

The real does conceptually not contain more than the possible. A hundred real dollars do conceptually not contain a penny more than a hundred possible dollars. . . . In my financial position no doubt there exists more by one hundred real dollars, than by their concept only, because in *reality* the object is not only contained analytically in my concept, but is added to my concept, synthetically; but the conceived hundred dollars are conceptually not in the least increased through the existence which is outside my concept. CPuR.

REASON The principle of private happiness would ruin morality altogether, were not the voice of reason so clear, so irrepressible, so distinctly audible, even to the commonest man. It can only, indeed, be maintained in the perplexing speculations of the schools, which are bold enough to shut their eyes against that heavenly voice, in order to support a theory that costs no trouble. CPrR.

186

Man really finds in himself a faculty by which he distinguishes himself from else, even from himself as affected by physical or nonreasonable objects, and that is nonphysical or spiritual Reason. **FM.**

Reason is the faculty of principles. **CPuR.**

Reason acts freely, without being determined in the chain of natural causes. **CPuR.**

The whole interest of my *reason*, whether theoretical or practical, is concentrated in the three following questions: 1. What can I know? 2. What should I do? 3. What may I hope? **CPuR.**

Reason is the faculty of deducing the particular from the general. **CPuR.**

Roused from every inquisitive indecision, as from a dream, by one glance at the wonders of nature and the majesty of the *cosmos*, reason soars from height to height till it reaches the highest, from the conditioned to conditions, till it reaches the supreme and unconditioned Author of all. **CPuR.**

In its moral use our supersensuous reason inevitably rises above the limits of *sensuousness*. **CPuR.**

Archimedes did not find a fixed point where reason could apply its lever: this fixed point is the idea of freedom supported by the moral law. **IK.**

REASON, CONCEPTS OF The *concepts of reason* are mere value ideas, and it is true that they have no object corresponding to them in experience; but they do not, for all that, refer to purely imaginary objects. **CPuR.**

REASON, PRACTICAL The distinction between the doctrine of happiness and the doctrine of morality is the first and most important office of the analytic of pure *practical reason.*
CPrR.

We have a concept of technical wisdom. We also get a conception of moral wisdom through our *practical reason.*
The Failure of all Philosophical Attempts
Towards a Theodicy.

REASON, PURE Since the oldest days of philosophy inquirers into the pure *reason* have conceived, besides the things of sense, or appearances, which make up the sensible world, certain objects of the pure understanding, which should constitute an intelligible world of reason.
PM.

REBELLION The subject can only lodge complaints but has no right to resistance or rebellion.
MM.

RECREATION Play is an occupation without a serious purpose, but it is refreshment from difficult work, a recreation.
LE.

REFLECTION Reflection is not concerned with objects themselves, in order to obtain directly concepts of them, but is a state of the mind in which we set ourselves to discover the subjective conditions under which we may arrive at concepts.
CPuR.

REGRESSUS If the conditioned is given, it imposes on us the regressus in the series of all conditions of it.
CPuR.
Vide Series.

REHABILITATION How it is possible that a man naturally bad should make himself a good man, transcends all our conceptions; for how can a bad tree bring forth good fruit? But since it is admitted that a tree originally good has brought forth bad fruit, the possibility of the contrary cannot be disputed. RR.

RELATION, CAUSAL The principle of the causal relation in the succession of phenomena is valid for all objects of experience. CPuR.

RELIGION Our bearing towards God must be characterized by reverence, love and fear—reverence for Him as a holy lawgiver, love for His beneficent rule, and fear of Him as a just judge. LE.

Religion must be practical. LE.

Morality as such is ideal, but religion imbues it with vigor, beauty, and reality. LE.

A judge trying a man for his life will not scoff at him: it is an important matter, the man's life is at stake and ridicule is out of place. So it is always with *religion*: whatever may be its particular absurdities in detail, it is no matter for ridicule. LE.

Religion is morality applied to God. It is ethics applied to *theology*. LE.

A religion which declares war on reason will not stand out against it for a long period. RR.

Religion is the recognition of all duties as divine commands. CPrR.

It is quite mistaken to fear that if we deprive religion of all that recommends it to the senses, it leads to mere cold assent. The contrary is true. Where the senses perceive nothing, the rule of *morality* rules alone. CJ.

189

RELIGIOUS STORIES Mere repeating of incomprehensible stories is certainly not a way to please God.   RR.

REMORSE A man often mistakes for remorse what is in fact a fear of the tribunal of justice. If, for instance, we slight some one in public we may reproach ourselves in the privacy of our home, but these are the reproaches of the Judge of Prudence within us, since we must suppose that we have made an enemy.   LE.

RENEGADE Whosoever renounces his religion is either a renegade or an apostate.   LE.

RENUNCIATION Our duty is renunciation, resignation to the will of God. We resign our will to another if we are conscious of his superior understanding and feel that his intentions are for our good.   LE. *Vide* Hypocrite.

REPENTANCE Repentance which manifests itself for the first time on the deathbed has no moral worth: its motive is the nearness of death; if the approach of death were not feared there would probably be no repentance. The penitent in such a case may be likened to the unlucky gambler who fumes and rages against himself for his folly and tears his hair. He has no qualms about the vice; he hates its consequence. We ought not to be misled into consoling and comforting a man for such a semblance of conscience. LE.

REPRESENTATION Understanding and sensibility [are] two totally distinct sources of representations.   CPuR.

REPRESENTATION, DARK If the consciousness is sufficient for distinguishing, but not for a consciousness of the difference, the representation would still have to be called dark.   CPuR. *Vide* Clearness.

REPROACH The reproach for an action through which damage arises is always a reproach of prudence. LE.

REPUBLICAN CONSTITUTION The republican constitution is the only one completely appropriate to human rights. But it is the most difficult to establish, because men with their selfish dispositions are incapable of a constitution of such sublime character. PP.

REPUTATION No man, be he ever so great, is indifferent to what others think of him. LE.

The man who is solicitous of his reputation may shrink from company so as not to risk incurring contempt, but the ambitious man cannot withdraw into solitude because he longs for the high esteem of others. LE.

RESERVE There is such a thing as a prudent reserve, which requires not silence but careful deliberation. LE.

RESERVATION Man is reserved in order to conceal faults and shortcomings. LE.

RESISTANCE Resistance, even against an allegedly unbearable misuse of the supreme power, is always illegal, because it would annihilate the entire legal constitution. MM.

RESPECT Respect applies always to persons only—not to things. The latter may arouse inclination, and if they are animals even love or fear; but never respect. CPrR.

If we wish to be respected we must respect others, we must respect humanity as a whole. LE.

RESPONSIBILITY Responsibility must be ascribed to man himself. RR.

191

Can we hold a man responsible for something which he does on the authority of the law? Can, for instance, a general be adjudged accountable for the death of enemy soldiers? Possibly for their death, but not for murder.   LE.

Responsibility presupposes free agency and a law.   LE.

What we have not done ourselves is hardly ours and we are not responsible for it.   RR.

REST Rest must be distinguished from idleness. . . . Rest cannot be properly enjoyed except after occupation.   LE.

RETIREMENT The man who retires and frees himself from all work does not feel nor enjoy his life.   LE.

REVERENCE We may honor a person outwardly, but reverence springs from the disposition of the heart.   LE.

REWARD No man can demand that God should reward him and make him happy. He may expect that God will see to it that he does not suffer for his good deeds, but reward must not be the impulsive ground of action.   LE.

To look on all *rewards* and punishments as merely the machinery in the hand of a higher power, which is to serve only to set rational creatures striving after their final end, this is to reduce the will to a mechanism destructive of freedom.   CPrR.

REWARD AND PUNISHMENT Rewards are more in harmony with morality than are punishments. Love is a stronger ground of impulse to performance. It is, therefore, better in religion to begin with reward rather than with punishment.   LE.

RICHES Riches ennoble a person's circumstances, but not himself. LE.

RIGHT Nature inexorably wants that the right should ultimately triumph. PP.

By war and its fortunate issue in *victory*, right is not decided. PP.

Rights are determined in *law*. LE.

Do not suffer your rights to be trampled underfoot by other persons with impunity. MM.

RIGHTS OF OTHERS There is nothing more sacred in the wide world than the rights of others. They are inviolable. Woe unto him who trespasses upon the right of another and tramples it underfoot! His right should be his security; it should be stronger than any shield or fortress. LE.

ROGUE As soon as *morality* is lacking in the least degree the man becomes a rogue. LE.

RULE An objective rule lays down what ought to occur, even though it never actually occurs. LE.

The representation of a general condition according to which something manifold *can* be arranged is called a rule, if it *must* be so arranged, a *law*. CPuR.

RULER The ruler cannot promote conciliation alone; men of all ranks in the state would have to be similarly trained; then would the state be built on a firm foundation. LE.

S

SABBATH The true sense of 'Sabbath' is not rest in general, but solemn rest. LE.

SACRIFICE It is better to sacrifice one's life than one's morality. To live is not a necessity; but to live honorably while life lasts is a necessity. LE.

SAGE The sage is happy in himself, he possesses all things, he has within himself the source of cheerfulness and righteousness, he is a king because he is lord of himself and, being his own master, he cannot be mastered. Such perfection could be attained only by strength in overcoming obstacles, and so a sage was regarded as even greater than the gods themselves, because a god had no temptations to withstand and no obstacles to overcome. LE.

SAVAGE Savages prefer senseless freedom to rational freedom. PP.

Savages who go about stark-naked, are cold towards each other. LE.

SAVING A man ought to be less saving in his old age than he was in his youth because he has fewer years of life to look forward to and will consequently need less. LE.

SCEPTICAL OBJECTION The sceptical objection places assertion and denial side by side, as of equal value, taking one or the other now as dogma, and now as denial; and being thus in appearance dogmatical on both sides, it renders every judgment on the object impossible. CPuR.

SCEPTICISM The sceptics are like nomadic tribes, who hate a permanent habitation. CPuR.

Scepticism is that artificial and scientific agnosticism which undermines the foundations of all knowledge, in order if possible to leave nothing trustworthy and certain anywhere. CPuR.

Scepticism makes short work with the whole of metaphysics. CPuR.

The sceptical manner of avoiding a troublesome business seems to be the shortest way out of all difficulties. CPuR.

Scepticism is a resting place of understanding, where it may reflect for a time on its dogmatical wanderings and gain a survey of the region where it happens to be, in order to choose its way with greater certainty for the future: but it can never be its permanent dwelling place. CPuR.

SCHOLAR For a scholar, thinking is a kind of food without which he cannot live, whether he learns from books or contemplates or invents. QuF.

Man is certainly not intended for learning only, and all of us cannot be scholars. Life is too short for that, and just as some are soldiers and some sailors, it is only some of us who ought to devote and dedicate ourselves to scholarship. LE.

Only scholars can judge of scholars. QuF.

196

Scholars follow their calling for the love of learning and not as a means of earning a fortune; they recognize that their profession is not a profitable, money-making business.

LE.

One scholar will not form a friendship of taste with another; because their capacities are identical; they cannot entertain or satisfy one another, for what one knows, the other knows too. But a scholar can form such a friendship with a businessman or a soldier. Provided the scholar is not a pedant and the businessman not a blockhead, each of them can talk entertainingly to the other about his own subject. LE.

The learned are seemingly the only class to observe the beauty which God has placed in the world. Can they not, therefore, claim superiority over their fellows? But listen to Rousseau; he turns the argument round and says: 'Man was not made for erudition, and scholars by their learning pervert the end of humanity.' What, then, are we to say? Rousseau is right up to a point, but when he goes on to talk of the damage that science does, he is badly at fault.

LE.

SCHOOLS The ridiculous despotism of the schools raises a loud clamor of public danger, whenever the cobwebs are swept away of which the public has never taken the slightest notice, and the loss of which it can therefore never perceive.

CPuR.

SCIENCE Without any love of honor, the sciences would lose their incentive. LE.

If science is to be advanced, all difficulties must be laid open, and we must even search for those that are hidden, for every difficulty calls forth a remedy, which cannot be discovered without science gaining either in extent or in

197

exactness; and thus even obstacles become means of increasing the thoroughness of science. CPrR.

Vide Concealment.

The sciences are principles for the betterment of morality. LE.

We do not enlarge, but we only disfigure the sciences, if we allow their respective limits to be confounded. CPuR.

SCIENTIFIC DIFFICULTIES If the scientific difficulties are intentionally concealed, or merely removed by palliatives, then sooner or later they burst out into incurable mischiefs, which bring science to ruin in an absolute scepticism. CPrR. *Vide* Disclosure.

SCOFFER The scoffer may be either scornful or mocking. An habitual scoffer betrays his lack of respect for others and his inability to judge things at their true value. LE.

SCORN Scorn is malicious. LE.

SECOND NATURE Place and custom form a second nature of which men are not conscious. A.

SECRETS Secrets have a way of coming out, and strength is required to prevent ourselves betraying them. A secret told is like a present given. LE.

Men who are not very talkative as a rule keep secrets well, but conversationalists who are at the same time clever, keep them better. The former might be induced to betray something, but the latter's gift of repartee invariably enables them to invent on the spur of the moment something non-committal. LE.

SECTS There are religious sects. These are associations formed

198

by men for the cultivation of their common religious views and sentiments. This is on the face of it a laudable purpose, but it tends to harden the heart against and to ostracize those who stand outside the pale of the particular sect. LE.

SELF Just as an innkeeper gives a thought to his own hunger when his customers have finished eating, so a man gives a thought to himself at the long last for fear that he might forget himself altogether. LE.

The *moral* self elevates man above himself. CPrR.

SELF-COMPULSION The more a man practices self-compulsion the freer he becomes. Some men are by nature more disposed to magnanimity, forgiveness, righteousness. It is easier for these to compel themselves and they are to that extent the freer. But no man is above self-compulsion. LE.

SELF-CONCEIT Self-conceit and dejection are the two rocks on which man is wrecked if he deviates, in the one direction or the other, from the moral law. On the one hand, man should not despair, but should believe himself strong enough to follow the moral law. On the other hand, he should avoid self-conceit and an exaggerated notion of his powers. LE.

SELF-CONFIDENCE We ought to show self-confidence and an air dégagé. A.

SELF-CONSCIOUSNESS Man is raised high above all other creatures by having the notion I; this is what makes him a person. A.

SELF-CONSTRAINT The concept of duty can contain no constraint except self-constraint, as far as the inner determination of the will is concerned. MM.

199

SELF-DEFILEMENT The thought of self-defilement is so revolting that even calling such a vice by its proper name is considered a kind of indecency. MM.

SELF-DESTRUCTION Man alters his ideal of happiness so often that nature could hardly cope with it. Moreover, with so many self-devised plagues, tyrannies, barbaric wars, he works at his own self-destruction. Our constitution is not made for happiness. CJ.

SELF-ESTEEM There is nothing unjust or unreasonable in self-esteem; we do no harm to another if we consider ourselves equal to him in our estimation. LE.

SELF-EXAMINATION This self-examination must be constant. LE.

SELF-FAVOR Self-favor should not be the principle of our duties towards ourselves. LE.

SELF-GOVERNMENT It is far better that man should so govern himself that he need gain no victory over himself. LE.

SELFISHNESS People who complain of lack of friends are those who are selfish and ever on the lookout to turn friendship to their own advantage. LE.

SELF-KNOWLEDGE The most difficult task of all duties, namely, self-knowledge. CPuR.

Moral self-knowledge, which attempts to fathom the scarcely penetrable depths of the heart, is the beginning of all human wisdom. Only the descent into the hell of self-knowledge paves the way for godliness. MM.

SELF-LOVE Self-love has two constituents, vanity and self-interest. Its aim is advantage to self; it is selfish and aims at satisfying our senses. LE.

So clear-cut are the frontiers between morality and self-love that even the coarsest eye cannot fail to notice it. CPrR.

SELF-MASTERY The principle of self-mastery is universal respect for one's own person in relation to the essential ends of humanity or human nature. LE.

SELF-OBLIGATION At first glance the concept of a duty to oneself contains a contradiction. But man can acknowledge a duty to himself without falling into self-contradiction, because the concept of man is not thought of in only one sense. The self-obligation, not being really a self-obligation, is not self-contradictory. Thus, the Fifth Antinomy can be solved. MM. *Vide* Judge.

SELF-RESTRAINT When a dog is hungry and there is food before him he must eat; man, however, in a similar situation, can restrain himself. LE.

SELF-REVELATION We all have a strong impulse to disclose ourselves, and enter wholly into fellowship; and such self-revelation is further a human necessity for the correction of our judgments. LE.

SELF-SEEKER He who is indifferent to the well-being of other men if only things go well with himself is a self-seeker. MM.

SELF-SURRENDER May a man mutilate his body for profit? May he sell a tooth? May he surrender himself at a price to the highest bidder? What is the moral aspect of such questions as these? LE.

SENILITY To be nursed in old age, avoid discomfort, refrain from going out in bad weather, let others do the work which one could do oneself—all this makes one prematurely senile. QuF.

SENSATION The effect produced by an object upon the faculty of representation so far as we are affected by it, is called sensation. CPuR.

A perception referring to the subject only, as a modification of his state, is sensation. CPuR.

Sensations can be intensified by contrast, novelty, change or gradual accretion. A.

SENSES Senses cannot think. CPuR.

We do not need panegyrics, merely advocates to defend the senses against their accusers. A.

Senses never err, not because they always judge rightly, but because they do not judge at all. CPuR.

SENSIBILITY This faculty of receiving representation according to the manner in which we are affected by objects, is called sensibility. CPuR.

SENSITIVITY Sensitivity has the power to admit pleasure and displeasure to the mind or to ward them off. A.

SENSUOUS The end of all sensuous things is a beginning for the nonsensuous beings who do not stand under the conditions of time and are subject to no other but moral destiny. ET.

SENTIMENTALITY Sentimentality is a weakness which allows others to play with our feelings as they choose. A.

SERGEANT A drill-sergeant calls down damnation upon the heads of his soldiers, not because he thinks that he can order the forces of damnation to do his bidding, but in order to add emphasis to his words of command.　　LE.

SERIES Everything that happens is only a continuation of the series, and no beginning is possible in it.　　CPuR.
Vide Regressus; Condition.

SERMONS We are for ever hearing sermons about what ought to be done from people who do not stop to consider whether what they preach can be done. As a result, the exhortations, which are tautological reiterations of the rule which everyone knows already, prove terribly boring. They express nothing that we are not already familiar with, and sermons consisting of such exhortations are very empty, unless the preacher has an eye to practical wisdom at the same time.　　LE.

SERVICE We can do a service to any individual, however great and important he may be; every subject can do an act of service to his superior.　　LE.

True service does not consist of observances and external usages: it is to be found in sanctified dispositions put into practice in our everyday activities.　　LE.

SEX The desire which a man has for a woman is not directed towards her because she is a human being, but because she is a woman; that she is a human being is of no concern to the man; only her sex is the object of his desires.　　LE.
Vide Cohabitation.

Each sex is ashamed of the vices of which its members are capable. Human beings feel, therefore, ashamed to mention those things of which it is shameful for humanity to be capable.　　LE.

SEX, FAIR He who first conceived of women under the name of the fair sex probably wanted to say something flattering, but he has hit upon it better than even he himself might have believed. **BS.**

SEXES Man must be manly and woman womanly; effeminacy in man pleases as little as does masculinity in woman. **LE.**

Difference of sex is more far-reaching than is usually believed. Men act from motives which are very different from those which actuate women. **LE.**

SEX IN MARRIAGE Even the permitted bodily union of the two sexes in *marriage* occasions much delicacy in higher circles, and requires a veil to be drawn over the subject whenever it must be mentioned. **MM.**

SEXUAL DESIRE Sexual desire is natural to all of us, yet we conceal it and make a secret of it; nature prompts us to this secrecy because by so doing we restrain this propensity or inclination, whereas if we were unabashed and talked openly about it, we should find it more difficult to keep it within bounds. **LE.**

SEX EDUCATION Rousseau asserts that it is a father's duty to give his son at the age of sixteen years a complete conception of sex and make no secret of it, clearing his mind in the subject and explaining the purpose of the desire and the harm that comes from the abuse of it. He must represent to him on moral grounds the heinousness of the abuse of sex, and show him the degradation of the worth of humanity in his own person which it entails. This is the last and most delicate point of education. **LE.**

SEXUAL INCLINATION The coarse feeling in the sexual inclination leads directly to the great purpose of nature; but because of its great universality it degenerates easily into excess and dissoluteness. BS.

SEXUALITY Sexuality exposes mankind to the danger of equality with the beasts. But as man has this desire from nature, the question arises how far he can properly make use of it without injury to his manhood. LE.

The end of humanity in respect of sexuality is to preserve the species without debasing the person. LE.

SEXUAL LOVE Sexual love makes of the loved person an object of appetite; as soon as that appetite has been stilled, the person is cast aside as one casts away a lemon which has been sucked dry. Sexual love can, of course, be combined with human love and so carry with it the characteristics of the latter, but taken by itself and for itself, it is nothing more than desire. LE.

SHALLOWNESS We often hear complaints against the shallowness of thought in our own time, and the decay of sound knowledge. But I do not see that sciences which rest on solid foundations, such as mathematics, physics, etc., deserve this reproach in the least. CPuR.

SHAME Sensitivity to shame is a secrecy of nature. BS.

No man feels shame for his piety and his fear of God, unless it be that he finds himself in wholly wicked and wholly defiant company; he is then ashamed of his conscience, in the way that one might feel ashamed of one's honesty among rogues; but in the company of moral men no one feels ashamed of being truly God-fearing. LE.

SICK What the sick man fancies is good for him. A.

SILENCE Silence is the readiest and most absolute method of reserve, but it is unsociable, and a silent man is not only unwanted in social circles but is also suspected.   LE.

SIMPLE, THE The simple can never occur in any experience, and the very possibility of a simple phenomenon is perfectly inconceivable.   CPuR.

SIMPLICITY Everything, the action of which can never be considered as the concurrence of several acting things, is simple.   CPuR.

SIN To be guilty of unnatural sins is to dishonor humanity in one's own person.   LE.

SINCERITY Truthfulness in one's statements is called honesty, and when these statements are at the same time promises, sincerity.   MM.

SIXTH SENSE There does exist an inclination which we may call an appetite for enjoying another human being. We refer to sexual impulse. This is the nature of a sense, which we can call the *sixth sense*.   LE.

SKILL The practical view refers to skill which is concerned with any contingent and casual ends.   CPuR.

SLANDERER The slanderer works surreptitiously: he speaks behind our backs; he must choose his company and we cannot overhear him.   LE.

SLEEP To sleep long or repeatedly saves much of the unpleasantness of life; but it is odd to wish for a long life and to spend it mostly asleep. To wake and sleep alternately during long winter nights is paralyzing and ruinous for the nervous system.   QuF.

During sleep some attention is still paid to the body; this

is why those who resolve in the evening to wake up earlier than usual indeed do so. QuF.

SMELL The least rewarding sense seems to be that of smell. A.

SNOBBERY Snobbery shows itself when a man gives himself airs and claims precedence, not on account of any intellectual or intrinsic merit, but on the ground of external appearances. The snob is vain in matters of social precedence, attaches importance to things which are of little account, and on any and every occasion, no matter how trifling, he claims the limelight. LE.

SOCIAL ENJOYMENT Every gathering implies a certain sacredness and duty of *discretion*. Without such trust all social enjoyment, so conducive to moral culture, would be destroyed. A.

SOCIAL INTERCOURSE In ordinary social intercourse and association we do not enter completely into the social relation. The greater part of our disposition is withheld; there is immediate outpouring of all our feelings, dispositions and judgments. We voice only the judgments that seem advisable in the circumstances. LE.

Social intercourse is in itself a cultivator of virtue and a preparation for its purer practice. LE.

SOCIAL SYSTEM As our social system is so arranged that we take part in the universal and open give and take of business with peculiar profit to ourselves, our acts of charity to others should not be regarded as acts of generosity, but as small efforts towards restoring the balance which the general social system has disturbed. LE.

SOCIETY The artificial conditions of society breed wags and sophists, but also fools and frauds. As artificiality grows, reason and virtue are accepted slogans; nice people eagerly talk about them, but can dispense with them. Anyway, better a rogue than a blockhead. DH.

SODOMY Sodomy is intercourse with animals. It degrades mankind below the level of animals, for no animal turns in this way from its own species. LE.

SOLDIER A soldier never knows how long and when he may be able to enjoy his fortune; he lives in uncertainty, and the soldier's profession is, moreover, very sociable. Thus there are no springs of avarice in him. LE.

SOPHISM Sophisms in arguments are most easily discovered, if they are put forward in a correct scholastic manner. CPuR.

SOPHIST A heedless sophist, in order to display his skill, would prove a proposition by plausible arguments and subvert the same immediately afterwards by arguments equally strong. CPuR.

The dogmatical sophists are deaf to all warnings of criticism. CPuR.

SOPHISTRY Sophistries at all events have the charm of novelty. CPuR.

SOUL The thinking substance as the principle of life in matter is the soul. CPuR.

SOUL, HUMAN If there is also an immaterial world, the human soul would have to be considered as belonging to two worlds at once, even in the present life. DS.

SOVEREIGNTY The idea of right has less authority with governments than the idea of independence and individual sovereignty, or the lust for despotic power. LE.

SPACE Space is not an empirical concept which has been derived from external experience. CPuR.

What experience teaches me is, that wheresoever I go, I always see before me a space in which I can proceed further. CPuR.

We only know substances in space through the forces which are active in a certain space, by either drawing others near to it or by preventing others from penetrating into it. CPuR.

SPACE AND TIME Space and time are only forms of sensuous intuition, therefore conditions of the existence of things as natural phenomena only. CPuR.

SPECIES Every species is always a concept containing that only which is common to different things, and as it cannot be completely determined, it cannot be directly referred to an individual, but must always comprehend other concepts, that is, sub-species. CPuR.

SPECIFICATION, LAW OF The law of specification imposes on the understanding the duty of looking for sub-species under every species, and for smaller varieties for every variety. CPuR.

SPECULATIVE I call a theoretical knowledge speculative, if it relates to a spiritual object which we can never reach in any sensuous experience. It is opposed to our knowledge of nature, which relates to a possible experience only. CPuR.

SPENDTHRIFT The spendthrift is incautious and improvident; he cannot know how long he will live, and having squandered what he had he may afterwards have to live in privation. LE. *Vide* Thrift.

SPIRITUALISM AND MATERIALISM On the one side pneumatism and on the other side materialism are opposed to dualism.　　　　　　　　　　　CPuR. *Vide* Dualism.

SPITE When a man would not grant to another even that for which he himself has no need, he is spiteful. Spite is a maliciousness of spirit.　　　　　　　　　　　　LE.

SPONTANEITY As it is impossible to arrive at a beginning of the conditions in causal relations, reason creates for itself the idea of spontaneity, or the power of beginning. CPuR.

SPY The spy arrogates to himself the right to watch the doings of strangers; no one ought to presume to do such a thing.
　　　　　　　　　　　　　　　　　　　　　　　　LE.

STANDARD We require a standard for measuring degree. The standard may be either natural or arbitrary.　　　　LE.

STANDARD OF CONDUCT Where this standard is employed as a measure of lesser quantities, it is an idea; when it is used as a pattern, it is an ideal.　　　　　　　　LE.

STATE The difficult problem of organizing a state can be solved even for a race of devils, if only they are intelligent.　PP.

States do not argue their cause before a tribunal; war alone is their way to present a plea.　　　　　　　　PP.

STEADFASTNESS The means for the cultivation of steadfastness of mind consists in the removal of that false appearance which lurks in the supposed goods of life and in the common acceptation of happiness.　　　　　LE.

STEPS OF UNDERSTANDING The first step in matters of pure understanding, which marks its infancy, is dogmatism. The second is scepticism, and marks the stage of caution on the part of understanding, when rendered wiser by experience. But the third step is necessary, that of the maturity and manhood of judgment, based on firm and universally applicable maxims. CPuR.

STRENGTH All strength is recognized only by the obstacles it can overcome. MM.

STROLLING Strolling in the open air should give relaxation by demanding a constant change of attention. QuF.

STUMBLING BLOCK Sorry though I should be to be a stumbling block to others, I could not help myself. LE.

STUPIDITY Deficiency in the faculty of *judgment* is really what we call stupidity, and there is no remedy for that. An obtuse and narrow mind, deficient in nothing but a proper degree of understanding and correct concepts, may be improved by study, so far as to become even learned. But as even then there is often a deficiency of judgment we often meet with very learned men, who in handling their learning betray that original deficiency which can never be mended. CPuR.

SUBSTANCE By substance we understand the permanent object of sensuous intuition. CPuR.

The coexistence of *substances* in space cannot be known in experience otherwise but under the supposition of reciprocal action. CPuR.

As an object of the pure understanding every substance must have internal determinations bearing on the internal reality. CPuR.

SUCCESSION In succession existence always comes and goes, and never assumes the slightest quantity. CPuR.

SUFFERING Man cannot be virtuous if he is not resolute in misfortune; in order to be virtuous he must be able to suffer.
LE.

SUICIDE Suicide can be regarded in various lights; it might be held to be reprehensible, or permissible, or even heroic.
LE.

We shrink in horror from *suicide* because all nature seeks its own preservation; an injured tree, a living body, an animal does so; how then could man make of his freedom, which is the acme of life and constitutes its worth, a principle for his own destruction?
LE.

Rage, passion and insanity are the most frequent causes of suicide, and that is why persons who attempt suicide and are saved from it are so terrified at their own act that they do not dare to repeat the attempt.
LE.

Suicide is immoral; for the intention is to rid oneself of all pains and discomforts attendant upon one's state by sacrificing that state, and this subordinates human nature to animal nature and brings the understanding under the control of animal impulses. In doing this I contradict myself, if I still desire to possess the rights of man.
LE.

SUMMUM BONUM Happiness in exact proportion with the morality of rational beings who are made worthy of happiness by it, constitutes alone the supreme good of a world into which we must necessarily place ourselves according to the commands of practical reason.
CPuR.

We may call this summum bonum an ideal, that is, the highest conceivable standard by which everything is to be judged and weighed.
LE.

212

SUPERSTITION Superstition is an irrational thing. Superstition is constantly creeping into religion.   **LE.**

An error is more excusable than a superstition in religion. Erroneous religion can be corrected, but a superstition is not only empty but is opposed to the reality of religion.   **LE.**

SUPREME BEING Time and labor are lost on the famous ontological proof of the existence of a Supreme Being from mere concepts; and a man might as well imagine that he could become richer in knowledge by mere ideas, as a merchant in capital, if, in order to improve his position, he were to add a few noughts to his cash account. **CPuR.**

SUPREME BEING The ideal of the *Supreme Being* is nothing but a regulative principle of reason.   **CPuR.**

The concept of a Supreme Being is, in many respects, a very useful idea.   **CPuR.**

Reason concludes that the Supreme Being, as the original or unconditioned ground of all things, must exist.   **CPuR.**

The first step which we take outside the world of sense, obliges us to begin our new knowledge with the investigation of the absolutely necessary Being, and to derive from its concepts the concepts of all things, so far as they are intelligible only.   **CPuR.**

SUPREME GOOD I call the idea of an intelligence in which the most perfect will, united to the highest blessedness, is the cause of all happiness in the world, so far as it corresponds exactly with morality, the ideal of the supreme good.   **CPuR.**

SUPREME GOVERNMENT The defender of religion confesses

SYLLOGISM Every syllogism is a form of deducing some kind of knowledge from a principle, because the major always contains a concept which enables us to know, according to a principle, everything that can be comprehended under the conditions of that concept. CPuR.

SYMBOLS Visible figures representing concepts are symbols. A.

Intellectually inferior persons can express themselves only in symbols. That accounts for the picturesque language we admire in savages. The splendor which we find in the ancient epics from Homer to Ossian, from Orpheus to the Prophets, is partly due to their lack of precise terms. A.

that if we can discover natural causes for all the order in the world, it is unnecessary to have recourse to a supreme world government. GTH.

SWEARING A great and wise moral legislator has entirely forbidden swearing as absurd and bordering on blasphemy. Heaven stands for the acme of happiness, hell for all that is bad, and the earth stands midway between these two extremes. LE.

SYMPATHY It is an indirect duty to cultivate our natural feelings for others, and to use them as so many means for sympathy based on moral principles. MM.

SYNCRETISM Syncretism is a form of sociability. It consists in agreeing with everyone for the sake of avoiding discord. It is very harmful. For he who agrees with everyone has no views at all. Let men err rather; for so long as they can distinguish one view from another, they can also be freed of their errors. LE. *Vide* Compromise.

SYNONYM Whenever there exists one single word only for a certain concept, we ought not be lavish in using it nor employ it, for the sake of variety only, as a *synonym* in the place of others, but carefully preserve its own peculiar meaning, as otherwise it may easily happen that the expression ceases to attract special attention, and loses itself in a crowd of other words of very different import, so that the thought, which that expression alone could have preserved, is lost with it. CPuR.

SYNTHESIS I understand by synthesis the act of arranging different representations together, and of comprehending what is manifold in them under one form of knowledge. CPuR.

SYNTHETICAL *Vide* Analytical and Synthetical.

SYSTEM If we review the entire extent of our *knowledge*, we shall find that it is the systematizing of that knowledge, that is, its coherence according to one principle, which forms the proper province of understanding . . . by which that knowledge becomes not only a mere aggregate but a system, connected according to necessary laws. CPuR.

SYSTEMATICAL UNITY The law of systematical unity requires that we should study nature as if there existed in it everywhere an infinitely systematical and well-planned unity. CPuR.

T

TALKATIVENESS Someone has said that women are talkative because the training of infants is their special charge, and their talkativeness soon teaches a child to speak, because they can chatter to it all day long. If men had to care for children, they would take much longer to learn to talk.
LE.

TASTE Taste contributes to social enjoyment and so long as it is not perverted, it judges the wholesomeness of a nutriment before it enters the stomach.
A.

Taste and color are by no means necessary conditions under which alone things can become to us objects of sensuous perception. They are connected with their appearance, as accidentally added effects only of our peculiar organization.
CPuR.

The *taste* of wine does not belong to the objective determinations of wine, considered as an object, but to the peculiar nature of the sense belonging to the subject that tastes the wine.
CPuR.

TAUTOLOGY A problem is tautologically resolved when conditions reappear in the solution which were already comprised in its statement. All practical sciences a priori, with the exception of mathematics, contain tautological propositions. Practical logic is full of them; it states conditions which have been stated by theoretical logic.
LE.

217

TAXES An overlord demands the payment of taxes: he does not demand that they should be paid willingly; ethics, however, demands that they should be so paid.   LE.

TEACHER OF WISDOM A teacher of wisdom would mean something more than a scholar who has not come so far as to guide himself, much less to guide others.   CPrR.

TELEOLOGY Teleology was meant to supplement the unity of nature according to general laws.   CPuR.

Moral teleology supplements the deficiencies of physical teleology.   CJ.

TEMPERAMENT A cold temperament is one which is unemotional and unmoved by love. A man whose spirit is never moved to impulses of kindness is said to be cold.   LE.

TEMPTATION Often enough we flatter ourselves that we are innocent though we have not withstood temptation. We have every reason to guard against temptation.   LE.

TEXTBOOK The chosen textbook must not be considered as a paragon of judgment; its statements are to be judged and criticized.   IK.

THANKFULNESS Universal nature, not particular circumstances, ought to evoke our thankfulness; for though the latter touches us more nearly, the former attitude is a nobler one.
          LE.

THEATRE PLAY Why are theatre plays so attractive? Because they keep us oscillating between anxiety and joy.   A.

THEFT There are animals who steal anything that comes their way, though it is quite useless to them; and it seems as if man had retained this animal tendency in his nature. LE.

If a starving man steals something from the dining room, the degree of his responsibility is diminished by the fact that it would have required great self-restraint for him not to do it. LE.

THEOLOGY Why do we need a theology at all? Clearly not in order to broaden our knowledge of nature. CJ.

The concept of such a being is the concept of God, and the ideal of pure reason is the object of theology. CPuR.

The being which contains the highest condition of the possibility of all that can be thought is the object-matter of theology. CPuR.

By theology we understand the knowledge of the original Being, derived either from reason only or from revelation. CPuR.

THING A thing is something which is incapable of any imputation. MM. *Vide* Person

THING IN ITSELF It would be absurd to admit no things in themselves. PM.

Natural phenomena are not things in themselves. CPuR.
Vide the Introduction.

THINKING We cannot say whether thinking can or cannot be done without a body. CJ.

In order to *know* an object, I must be able to prove its possibility, either from its sensuous reality, or by means of spiritual reason. But I can *think* whatever I please, provided only I do not contradict myself. CPuR.

THOROUGHNESS I have observed with pleasure and thankfulness in various publications that the spirit of thoroughness is

219

not yet dead in Germany, but has only been silenced for a short time by the clamor of a fashionable and pretentious license of thought.   CPuR.

THOUGHT I recognize in me thoughts which I ascribe to a non-material being.   DS.

Thought is the act of referring a given intuition to an object.   CPuR.

Thoughts without contents are empty, intuitions without concepts are blind.   CPuR.

I believe that in our sleep, when the external senses are completely at rest, our thoughts are clearer and more comprehensive than in our waking hours. However, the sensation of the body is not felt at the same time and does not accompany the *dream*.   DS.

THREAT Threats do not impose an obligation, they extort. LE.

THRIFT Thrift is care and scruple in the spending of one's substance. It is no virtue; it requires neither skill nor talent. A spendthrift of good taste requires much more of these qualities than does he who merely saves. The thrifty, who acquire their wealth by saving, are as a rule small-minded people, but amongst the spendthrifts we find men of spirit and high intelligence.   LE.

TIME The more attention we give to time, the more we feel that it is empty. Thus, for instance, when we watch the clock, time becomes long. But he who has something to do, does not notice time and it appears to him shorter. LE.

The human mind abhors an empty time, and is bored and disgusted with it.   LE.

Time cannot be perceived externally, as little as space can be perceived as something within us. CPuR.

The three modi of time are permanence, succession, and coexistence. CPuR.

TOBACCO Tobacco causes first an unpleasant sensation, which, however, is at once canceled out by salivary secretion and thus becomes almost company, supplying ever new sensations and even thoughts. A.

There are certain stimuli, such as *tobacco*, which can be enjoyed the whole day long without producing satiation. A.

TOLERANCE Tolerance is a universal human duty. Men have many defects, real and apparent, but we must endure them. In matters of religion we show our tolerance by contemplating without hatred religious views which we dislike and which we regard as defective or mistaken. Why should I hate a man because he holds to be true something which according to my own religion is untrue? LE.

TRAGEDY Tragedy is distinguished from comedy chiefly in that in the first the feeling for the sublime is stirred, and in the second, that for the beautiful. BS.

TRANSCENDENT All principles which tend to transgress the limits of possible experience, we shall call transcendent. CPuR.

TRANSCENDENT IDEA *Vide* Ideas, transcendent.

TRANSCENDENTAL Transcendental, that is, independent of empirical principles. CPuR.

I call all knowledge transcendental which is occupied not so much with objects, as with our manner of knowing ob-

221

jects, so far as this is meant to be possible a priori. A system of such concepts might be called Transcendental Philosophy. CPuR. *Vide* A priori.

TRANSCENDENTAL IDEA Transcendental or moral ideas have a most admirable and indispensably necessary regulative use. CPuR.

The transcendental or moral ideas will probably possess their own proper and, therefore, immanent use, although, if their object is misunderstood, and they are mistaken for the concepts of real things, they may become transcendent in their application, and hence deceptive. CPuR.

TRANSCENDENTAL PHILOSOPHY Transcendental philosophy is a system of all principles of pure reason. CPuR. *Vide* Transcendental.

TRANSCENDENTAL PREDICATE Necessity, infinity, unity, extramundane existence, eternity, freedom from conditions of time, omnipresence, freedom from conditions of space, omnipotence, etc., all these are transcendental predicates. CPuR.

TRANSCENDENTAL QUESTION Transcendental questions admit of transcendental answers only, that is, of such which consists of mere concepts without any empirical admixture. CPuR.

TRANSCENDENTAL REASON We regard transcendental reason, in spite of all empirical conditions, as completely free. CPuR.

TRANSGRESSION Every transgression has a penal desert for the reason that it has been committed. LE.

TRAVELING Traveling enlarges our horizon, but in order to

222

know what to look for abroad, we should first acquire some knowledge of our fellows in town and country.   **A.**
Vide Kant's Birthplace.

TREATISE At single points every philosophical treatise may be pricked, while yet the organic structure of the system, considered as a whole, has not therefore to apprehend the slightest danger.   CPuR.

TROUBLE It is better to bear one's own troubles than to bother others with them.   LE.

TRUTH What is truth? is an old question by which people thought they could drive logicians into a corner, and either make them take refuge in a mere circle, or make them confess their ignorance and consequently the vanity of their whole art. The nominal definition of truth, that it is the agreement of the cognition with its object, is granted.   CPuR.

The purely logical criterion of truth, namely, the agreement of knowledge with the general and formal laws of the understanding, is no doubt a negative condition of all truth.
CPuR.

We do not seem to be content with hearing only what is true, but want to know a great deal more.   CPuR.

It is the country of truth but surrounded by a wide and stormy ocean, the true home of illusion, where many a fog bank and ice that soon melts away tempt us to believe in new lands, while constantly deceiving the adventurous mariner with vain hopes, and involving him in adventures which he can never leave, and yet can never bring to an end.   CPuR.

Without *truth* social intercourse and conversation become valueless.   LE.

223

One truth is consistent with another. On the other hand, lies contradict each other and are inconsistent with my purposes and with those of others. LE.

The systematical unity of the knowledge is the touchstone of the *truth*. CPuR.

Subtle errors are alluring to men's self-assurance, manifest truths share the fate of those songs which one can no longer endure when they resound from the mouth of the common people; briefly: certain propositions are appreciated not because they are correct but because they cost us much and one does not like to acquire truths as a cheap bargain. Some Reflections on Optimism.

TRUTHFULNESS If we were to be at all times punctiliously truthful we might often become victims of the wickedness of others who were ready to abuse our truthfulness. LE.

U

UNCONDITIONED The word *unconditioned* is used, in order to get rid of all the conditions which the *understanding* always requires, when wishing to conceive something as necessary. CPuR.

The determination of the causality of beings in the world of *sense* can never be unconditioned; and yet there must be something unconditioned. Hence, the idea of freedom. CPrR.

That which impels us by necessity to go beyond all conditioned phenomena, is the unconditioned, which understanding postulates in all things by themselves. CPuR.

UNCONDITIONED NECESSITY The being the concept of which contains a therefore for every wherefore, which is in no point and no respect defective, and is sufficient as a perfect condition everywhere, is not capable of any condition, and satisfies at least in this respect the concept of unconditioned necessity. CPuR.

UNDERSTANDING Understanding, holding in one hand its principles, according to which concordant phenomena alone can be admitted as laws of nature, and in the other hand the experiment, which it has devised according to those principles, must approach nature, in order to be taught by it: but not in the character of a pupil, who agrees to everything the master likes, but as an appointed judge, who compels the witnesses to answer the questions which he himself proposes. CPuR.

We shall call this formal and pure condition of sensibility, to which the concept of understanding is restricted in its application, its schema; and the function of the understanding in these schemata, the schematism of the pure *understanding*. CPuR.

If the understanding cannot decide whether certain questions lie within its own horizon or not, it can never feel certain with regard to its claims and possessions, but must be prepared for many humiliating corrections, when constantly transgressing, as it certainly will, the limits of its own domain, and losing itself in follies and fancies. CPuR.

It is by no means unusual, in ordinary conversations, as well as in written works, that by carefully comparing the thoughts uttered by an author on his own subject, we succeeded in understanding him better than he understood himself, [if] he did not sufficiently define his concept, and thus not only spoke, but sometimes even thought, in opposition to his own intentions. CPuR.

The understanding may be defined as the faculty of judging. CPuR.

The understanding knows all that it knows by concepts only. CPuR.

Understanding follows its own course in its empirical use, and again a peculiar course in its transcendental use. CPuR.

UNDERSTANDING, SCHEMATISM OF The concept of dog means a rule according to which my imagination can always draw a general outline of the figure of a four-footed animal, without being restricted to any particular figure supplied by experience. This schematism of our understanding is an art hidden in the depth of the human soul.   CPuR.

Vide Schematism.

UNIFORMITY Uniformity can only result when all men act according to the same principle.   OE.

UNITY The unity of the universe is evidently a mere deduction of the quietly adopted principle of the communion of all substances as coexistent; for if they were isolated, they would not form parts of a whole.   CPuR.

Unity of reason is never the unity of a possible experience, but essentially different from it, as the unity of the understanding.   CPuR.

All transcendental ideas can be arranged in three classes: the first containing the absolute unity of the thinking subject; the second the absolute unity of the series of conditions of natural phenomena; the third the absolute unity of the condition of all objects of thought in general. CPuR.

UNIVERSALITY Universality is the absolute allness of the appertaining parts.   DFP.

UNIVERSE, ORIGIN OF The attempt to derive the formation of the celestial bodies from the first primitive state of nature by mechanical laws seems to go far beyond the limits of human understanding.   GTH.

V

VALUE To the man who wants money to spend, it is all the same whether the gold was dug out of the mountain or washed out of the sand, provided it is accepted at the same *value*.
CPrR.

Skills and diligence in work have a market price; wit, imagination, whims have fancy *value*.
FM.

VALUE AND DIGNITY Whatever has reference to the inclinanations and wants of mankind has a market *value*; but that which constitutes the condition under which alone anything can be an end in itself, this has dignity.
IK.

VALUE IDEA A concept formed of notions and transcending all possible sensuous experience is a value idea, or a concept of reason.
CPuR.

It must be extremely irksome to hear the value free representation of red color called a value idea.
CPuR.

VANITY To aim at gaining respect by dress, or by titles, or by any other things which are not inherent in our person, is vanity.
LE.

VENGEANCE Vengeance is not synonymous with claiming one's rights.
LE.

VERBOSITY The precocious verbosity of young thinkers is blinder than any other concept and more incurable than ignorance.   IK.

Verbosity — that defect of *old age* which is usually not seriously blamed but merely smiled at.   QuF.

VERSIFICATION Versification without spirit is not *poetry*.   A.

VICE Vices bring their own *punishment*.   LE.

VILENESS The three vices which are the essence of vileness and wickedness are *ingratitude*, envy, and malice.   LE.

VIRTUE There must be a virtue in man. Therefore we must believe in virtue.   LE.

Moral unbelief is *disbelief* in the actuality of virtue. It is an evil thing to throw doubt upon the existence of virtue, the germ of good in man. Many learned men have done so in order to bring home to men their degeneracy, and to disabuse them of the notion that they are virtuous. It is none the less a hateful expedient.   LE.

Virtue pleases uniquely but it does not satisfy; if it did, all men would be virtuous. His very virtue intensifies a man's yearning for happiness. The more virtuous and the less happy a man is, the more painful is the feeling that he is not happy, though deserving *happiness*. Such a man is satisfied with his conduct, but not with his condition. LE.

Virtue is a glorious word. It signifies courage and bravery.   RR.

Virtue is always in progress and yet always begins at the beginning.   MM.

That no man can ever act up to the pure idea of virtue, does not in the least prove the chimerical nature of that concept; for every judgment as to the moral worth or unworth of actions is possible by means of that idea only.

CPuR.

VIVISECTION Vivisectionists, who use living animals for their experiments, certainly act cruelly, although their aim is praiseworthy, and they can justify their cruelty, since animals must be regarded as man's instruments; but any such cruelty for sport cannot be justified. LE.

Man is entitled to kill animals quickly and painlessly or to make them do hard work, as long as it is not beyond their strength. However, excruciating experiments for the sake of mere speculation are to be abhorred. MM.

VOTE The right to vote which gives a man his qualifications as a citizen presupposes self-sufficiency. MM.

W

WAG A wag who, apparently serious, excites a lively expectation and then releases it abruptly like a stretched string, provokes a healthy vibration of the digestive muscles.   A.

WANTS The more plentiful nature's gifts and the greater our store of the world's goods the greater are our wants. With growing wealth we acquire fresh wants, and the more we satisfy them the keener becomes our appetite for more. So our hearts are restless for ever.   LE.

We have wants, and these wants control the matter of our desires.   CPrR.

WAR War cancels out all progress.   QuF.

War implies no special motive but appears to be implanted in human nature; it passes even for something noble, to which the love of glory induces men quite apart from any selfish incentive.   PP.

WARMTH I cannot confirm that 'one should keep one's head and feet warm'; better keep them both cool to avoid catching a cold.   QuF.

WEAKNESS When we talk of the weakness of human nature we mean its lack of the degree of moral goodness.   LE.

233

WEALTH Of the wealthy man we ask to what use he intends to put all those treasures which he has in plenty. LE.

A wealthy man is highly esteemed by his fellows because of his wealth; a needy man is less respected because of his straitened circumstances. LE.

WEIGHT A philosopher was asked, What is the weight of smoke? He replied, Deduct from the weight of the wood burnt the weight of the remaining ashes, and you have the weight of the smoke. He was therefore convinced that even in fire matter does not perish, but that its form only suffers a change. CPuR.

WELL-BEING The physical good or well-being, for which health and wealth are requisite, is not by itself the greatest good; the ethical good, right conduct, worthiness of being happy, must be added to the former. LE.

WELL-WISHING Mere well-wishing is only a considerate regard for the well-being of other persons without one's having to contribute anything to it. MM.

WHISPERING If I see two people whispering to each other so as not be heard, my inclination ought to be to get further away so that no sound may reach my ears. LE.

WHITE LIE As men are malicious, it cannot be denied that to be punctiliously truthful is often dangerous. This has given rise to the conception of a white lie, the lie enforced upon us by necessity—a difficult point for moral philosophers. For if necessity is urged as an excuse it might be urged to justify stealing, cheating and killing, and the whole basis of morality goes by the board. Then, again, what is necessity? LE.

WICKED Even the wicked have rules of conduct. LE.

WIFE In domestic matters, scholars like often to be treated as minors by their wives. **A.**

WILL To will is to have a desire which is within our own control. **LE.** *Vide* Wish; Free Will.

Intelligence, wit, judgment, and the other talents of the mind are undoubtedly good and desirable in many respects; but these gifts of nature may also become extremely bad and mischievous if the will which is to make use of them, is not good. **FM.**

WISDOM Wisdom consists more in conduct than in knowledge. **FM.**

We cannot say of wisdom, as if contempuously, that it is an idea only, but for the very reason that it contains the idea of the necessary unity of all possible aims, it must determine all practical acts, as an original and, at least, limitative condition. **CPuR.**

WISE MAN Virtue and human wisdom in its perfect purity are ideas, while the wise man is an ideal, that is, a man existing in thought only, but in complete agreement with the idea of wisdom. **CPuR.**

WISH To wish is to have a desire which is not within our control. **LE.**

WIT Who has always his wits about him? **MM.**

The wit sufficient for composing a book is not enough to produce and enliven ideas concerning important business. **A.**

Wit is humorous if it grows out of a liking for paradoxes. **A.**

WOMEN All women are minors in law. The husband is their natural guardian. Although when it comes to talking, women are decidedly 'major' to men and would be quite able to plead for themselves. A.

Women have a strong inborn feeling for all that is beautiful, elegant, and decorative. BS.

WONDER The sublime feeling is sometimes accompanied with a certain dread, or melancholy; in some cases merely with quiet wonder; and in still others with a beauty completely pervading a sublime plan. BS.

WORD Those whose minds are practiced in harboring ideas and dispositions can discard the aid of words and formal expressions. LE.

WORK Why is work the best means for enjoying life? Because tiresome labor which rewards only by its success, creates joy and well-being through its mere disappearance. A.

Work is useful occupation with a purpose. The loftier its purpose the greater the difficulties and hardships of work. Man must be active and industrious and must undertake difficult work readily and cheerfully; otherwise his work will bear the marks of compulsion, and not of facility. LE.

Man feels more contented after heavy work than when he has done no work; for by work he has set his powers in motion; he, therefore, feels them better, and his mind is on that account more alive to pleasure. LE.

Work is an incentive to virtue. LE.

WORLD The world is a sum of phenomena. CPuR.

I call the world, in so far as it may be in accordance with

moral laws, a moral world (in contradistinction to the natural or amoral world). CPuR.

WORSHIP The more worship is overloaded with observance, the more devoid it is of moral exercises. Religious worship is no direct service of God: it is only a means of exercising the human mind in dispositions to behave in all things in accordance with God's will, and in that lies its value. LE.

WRETCHEDNESS Wretchedness and misery are our own fault. LE.

WRONGING It is not enough to say that we have never wronged a man; for we may have done wrong in general. LE.

Y

YOUTH Youth is less inclined to be miserly than old age. Youth has the possibility open to it of acquiring almost anything, but not so old age. LE.

Nothing would prove in the long run more vain and inefficient than to keep the reason of youth in temporary tutelage, and to guard it against temptation for a time at least. CPuR.

Z

ZEAL Zeal is a resolute and steadfast will to pursue ˌof set purpose and to reach the aim in view. Such zeal is commendable in all things; but if in religion it signifies a passionate pursuit of everything in it, then it is blind zeal; and if in anything in life we should keep our eyes open it is in religion. In religion, therefore, there is no room for zeal, but only for serious determination. **LE.**

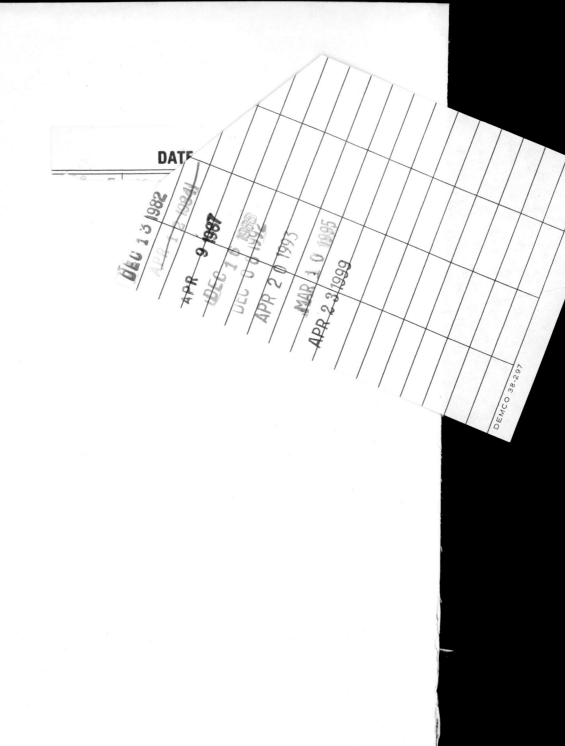